how to trust **God**

how to trust **God**

when *life* doesn't make **sense**

GARY R MAYES

Crossway Books

CROSSWAY BOOKS
38 De Montfort Street, Leicester LE1 7GP, England

Originally published as *Now What!* by Crossway Books, a division
of Good News Publishers, Wheaton, Illinois 60187, USA.

This edition published by arrangement with Good News Publishers.

First British edition 1996

British Library Cataloguing in Publication Data.
A catalogue record for this book is available from the British Library.

ISBN 1-85684-143-X

Typeset in the United States of America
Printed in Great Britain by
Cox and Wyman Ltd, Reading, Berks

To Margaret

you are my padded cell
my constant encouragement
my partner in all things
and my best friend

Table of Contents

Introduction

If you are at all like me, you are weary of books with simple formulas and humanly concocted solutions to the stresses and anxieties of life. You long to discover eternally valid insights from Scripture for those seasons when life doesn't make sense. This is a book that shares your passion for biblically-based principles and patterns that can lead to the discovery of genuine rest.

Rest . . . Although it is a familiar word, on many days it seems to be a foreign commodity. Yet, it is something we all crave deep down inside. One syllable bearing a lifetime of significance. Rest.

I don't mean the rest of physical inactivity, but a condition of spirit. The ability to maintain an even keel in the midst of raging seas. The calm center that provides perspective when the urgent demands of life are blaring and relentless.

Each of us knows what it is to trudge through difficult and demanding circumstances that are far beyond our control. Circumstances that make no sense can cripple our faith, distort our perspective on life, and plague us with doubts about God's ability or interest. We know what it is to be dealt a real-world "Go to jail" card—to be sidelined unexpectedly, to be trapped before a demanding and inescapable decision. We know what it is to be stuck for extended periods of time in circumstances that give us no option but to wait. With the passing of time these waiting room experiences stretch the ligaments of our faith to the breaking point and beyond.

Like it or not, life is filled with seasons that make no sense. It seems everyone experiences them. Times when circumstances are anything but what we wish they were and remain beyond our control. We fear the future and are confused by the present. We look to the Lord, but He seems either silent or drowned out by the winds howling around us. The internal nature of the pressures, anxieties, fears, and doubts we face can cause us to feel alone, even abandoned.

You may be there right now. If you aren't, I am certain you have been in the past, perhaps even recently. And I am certain you will return in the future. In fact, it seems that at any given moment all of us have at least one area in our lives where the pieces don't make sense, where we are waiting for God's direction and/or intervention. These are seasons of life that demand timeless and eternally relevant answers from God and His Word.

This book was born in just such a time in my life. The difficulty of my journey was only surpassed by the grace and power of God's Word and the intimacy that is born out of desperate dependency on Him.

Therefore, I invite you to embark on a journey. Not a rehashing of my journey, but a journey of your own as you discover how rich and profound God's words are for you. You will revisit old friends whose portraits include the flaws of real life. You will explore insights and answers that have stood the test of time.

To guide your journey through this book, the chapters are divided into three major sections, each section tackling the issues from a different angle, each building upon the lessons of the others. To help you gain your bearings, here is a brief look at the focus for each of the three sections.

Part One:
SECRETS OF REST
Because we need principles to guide our steps.

Rest can be as elusive as trying to nail Jell-O to the wall. Just when we think we have it nailed down, the changing wind of our circumstances causes it to wriggle loose. Just as we begin to taste genuine rest, we find ourselves scrambling after it again. This section of the book takes us to the source and explores principles and patterns outlined in Scripture that lead to rest. These chapters will give direction and focus to your relationship with the Lord during difficult days.

Part Two:
ENEMIES OF REST
Because we need to be prepared for the battles we'll face.

Wise adversaries know that the frontal attack is rarely the wisest move. Rather, they attack from the rear or from the side. And if possible, they sabotage from within. The enemies of rest are no different. They attack from the inside, for the greatest enemies of rest are not external but internal. Impatience, discontent, and discouragement build up steam, unnoticed at first, but then spring upon us with brutal force.

In every case these enemies tempt us to compromise our convictions. They fog our thinking and occupy us with delusions of self-sufficiency. They lure us into rationalizing away our priorities. They generate powerful doubts about God's character and attempt to short-circuit our faith.

You will meet these enemies face to face in this section and will explore your options for responding to their attacks.

Part Three:
COMPANIONS ON OUR SEARCH FOR REST
Because we need people to walk beside us.

When the circumstances of life don't make sense, we often feel very alone. The best answers and insights can sound hollow when the screaming demands of life surround us. For that reason, you may find that this is the richest section of the book.

James 5:17 tells us that Elijah (and by implication, all the men and women in the Scriptures) was just like us. These individuals were people who faced life just as we do and encountered the same intense challenges confronting us. If we look hard we can see ourselves in their circumstances. Their names may be Abraham, Joseph, Esther, David, or Paul; but beneath the surface we can see dynamics identical to those we face.

To that end, this section offers a smattering of companions from Scripture, partners who will walk with us and give us hope. People who have been where we are and discovered what it is to have the Lord carry their burden. People who discovered intimacy with God during moments when the pieces of life were broken around them. You will gain a whole new appreciation for these individuals. They will no longer be men and women of history, but partners who will walk beside you and offer you hope.

The depth of our need may feel bottomless at times. But the fruit of this journey in my own life has taught me that no matter how great my need, God's provision runs greater.

I have discovered that in the midst of brokenness and need, intimacy with Jesus Christ is more readily available than ever.

More than anything else, I pray that you will discover a rest in your spirit that grows out of increased relationship with the Lord Jesus Christ. His presence and power transcend the demands of your circumstances and can become a calm center in the midst of life's whirlwinds. As you stand in the midst of the rubble caused by circumstances that make no sense, I pray that you will discover intimacy with Jesus in a new way.

GARY MAYES
April 1995

PART ONE

SECRETS OF REST

*Because we
need principles to
guide our steps*

CHAPTER ONE

An Ancient Prescription

Brad walked through the front door about six o'clock, about the time he did almost every day. Dropping his sport coat, the newspaper, and a few papers from work onto his favorite chair, he couldn't wait to greet his bride and swap stories about the day. Today's commute home in the crisp autumn air past newly strung Christmas lights had put him in an especially good mood, eager to spend a quiet evening with his wife.

Although Brad and Darlene had been married ten years, they still cherished this daily reunion as intensely as if they were newlyweds. Perhaps the absence of children in their home kept their attentions focused on one another. Or perhaps the frustration and heartbreak resulting from their inability to have children had driven them toward a deeper sense of partnership. At any rate, on most days Darlene was home before Brad and puttering around downstairs awaiting his return. Not today.

Within moments after his arrival, Brad noticed the house was conspicuously quiet. Darlene's Honda was in the garage, her purse was on the kitchen table, lights were on, but there was no sign indicating where she was. There was no note or message of any kind. "Where could she be?" Brad wondered aloud. Then he heard the sound of muffled sobs coming from the bedroom upstairs.

Darlene sat huddled in the middle of their bed, surrounded by opened Christmas letters now strewn around her. Her puffy eyes and running mascara and the growing pile of crumpled tissues told the story without a word. Every year about this time the sleeping giant of disappointment over their inability to have children awoke. Christmas letters from scattered friends were so upbeat and overflowing with news about growing children that Darlene felt a twisting jab with each one she read.

Most of their friends were impressed by the external contentment Brad and Darlene displayed in spite of how desperately they wanted children. They had never hidden their desire for children of their own and always appeared hopeful about their future prospects. However, their sleeping giant of disappointment never went away. At times he dozed innocently and appeared tame. At other times the slightest unexpected event awoke this villain, causing him to roar and flail and tear into the same lingering wound felt by thousands of childless couples.

At moments like this for Brad and Darlene—and for anyone who wrestles with unanswered prayer, unresolved problems, unattainable dreams, or other situations that lead to stress and anxiety—piercing, unnerving questions rage at a furious pace. Will God ever answer my prayer? Has God forgotten me? Am I supposed to keep waiting forever? How in the world can I be content when I am stuck with this burden? Am I doing something wrong? What if my faith fails under the pressure? What about God's promise that He will not let me face anything I am not strong enough to handle?

Brad and Darlene's situation is not unique. It is an experience shared by thousands of couples. The types of questions they wrestle with are not unique either. Their situation is one of childlessness, but you may find yourself struggling in an identical way over completely dissimilar circumstances.

The landscape of your life may appear quite distinct from Brad and Darlene's situation. But the common experience we all share when buried by circumstances beyond our control is the same feeling of helplessness and anxiety. We crave for a sense of rest, a calm center to transcend the swirling storm around us. We long for a deep faith that can stare down any cause for alarm with undaunted security and strength. Whether the events we face are major life crises, relational conflicts that seem irreconcilable, an urgent or risky personal decision, an economic dilemma we cannot resolve, or any number of other concerns, when life locks us in the waiting room we yearn for the rest and peace that passes all understanding. We yearn for that internal quality of rest that can steady our life during the most turbulent of times.

This book is written to explore the timeless secrets of Scripture that provide in-depth encouragement for our lives when circumstances do not make sense. This book is written for the Brads and Darlenes—for all of us who face troubling circumstances and crave secrets that will guide our steps and guard our hearts.

A CALM CENTER

Warning: These secrets we are about to explore are internal, not external. They have little to do with manipulating our circumstances and everything to do with nurturing a calm center in our lives. They are based on the changeless character of God rather than on success in changing our circumstances. When applied, these secrets have the power to measurably change our lives whether the world around us changes or not.

What does it take to find authentic rest that flows from the inside out? The key is to search for rest in the right place. Genuine rest is often so elusive because we expect to find it linked with circumstances. After all, if changing circumstances are the apparent cause of our unrest, it would seem logical to believe that better circumstances are essential to renewed rest.

However, if internal rest is only possible with improved circumstances, people like Brad and Darlene have nothing to carry them through the demands of the present but their ability to tough things out. They would have no hope for bona fide rest unless a child enters the picture.

Actually, a calm center is possible even in the most difficult of circumstances.

You have seen this principle in action. All of us have known folks who managed to experience peace and rest while stuck in high-pressure situations. We have watched and spoken with friends who were honestly at peace even as their lives swirled in major-league crisis. On the other hand, we have also known people to become completely demoralized by encounters with temporary, little-league problems.

External circumstances are not the key to experiencing rest. The internal condition of our *heart* is the key. I would call this a calm center. The presence or absence of rest at the center of our lives determines the manner and extent to which we are shaken by the circumstances of life. Therefore, our quest is to identify what we can do to cultivate this calm center, this fountainhead of rest.

Using only four words, God identifies the divine prescription for cultivating that calm center: *Wait on the Lord*.

Waiting on the Lord encompasses a wide range of qualities: trust, endurance, patience, and submission, to name only a few. But perhaps waiting on Him connects so well with us because it immediately implies the issue of timing. Stress and anxiety are always connected to time. Always. Whether the problem we face relates to the quantity of time that has passed, the brevity of time remaining, or the actual timing of the problem, time is always a factor.

At the heart of it all, we are desperate for rest that can carry us through the circumstances of life. We crave for God to create a fountain at the core of our being that will overflow with waters of rest and peace. By definition that means we need to abandon the notion that our circumstances must change.

Transformation on the inside is what we need, and the ancient prescription of waiting on the Lord is God's contemporary offer to meet this need. It is a simple formula, really—an invitation to renewal. It's an invitation to internal renovation in spite of our circumstances. Listen to God as He speaks for Himself:

> *Those who* wait for the Lord *will gain new strength;*
> *they will mount up with wings like eagles, they will run*
> *and not get tired, they will walk and not become weary.*
>
> (Isaiah 40:31, NASB, emphasis added)

He invites us to rest in faith when solutions remain unseen. He invites us to trust in His timetable in spite of the way it differs from our own. He offers to take the weight of our burdens and place them upon His own able shoulders. He offers to replace our anxiety with His peace, our stress with His rest, and our weariness with His strength. His offer is wrapped in those four simple words, "Wait for the Lord."

WHAT STANDS IN OUR WAY

Before we get ahead of ourselves, it is crucial for us to examine the obstacles we must overcome on this journey. A long-understood axiom of healthy problem-solving is: first, accurately define the problem at hand. We need a firm grasp on those forces that battle against personal victory in this area. Therefore, we will begin our journey by taking a few steps backwards and looking at the forces we are up against.

Obviously, we are impatient people. And this personal struggle with impatience is inflamed by the influence of our "go-for-it-now" society. The insidious impact that the world has on our lives in general and on our relationship with God in particular demands a closer look.

Three prevalent and devastating lies affect us continually. They are bold but untrue. Yet they are heard or felt so frequently that we act as if they were true. They rip apart our ability to rest in God's hands. And they radically undermine our confidence in God's game plan.

Lie #1: "You Can Have It All!"

How often are you bombarded by messages making this claim? You'll hear, "Hey, you deserve it all." "If you don't have the money today that's OK, because for no money down and no interest for ninety days you can acquire just about any handy item you need." "With this credit card you can purchase more than you can afford in almost any country on the globe."

Don't get me wrong—this is not a commentary on fiscal responsibility, but a simple reminder of the frequency and intensity of this lie. It doesn't matter how often you hear this claim, *it is not true!* You cannot have it all. No one can.

Lie #2: "You Can Have It All Now!"

In addition to the lie that says we can have it all, we are pressured to believe we can have it all *now*!

Come on, be real! This isn't true now, nor has it ever been. Sure, we benefit from many inventions not available to preceding generations. Television and radio have given us instant access to news from around the world. Computers have made an amazing impact. For example, they speed up the work of Bible translation in the most remote locations on the globe. And as much as we decry the invasion of fast food, think about how often a hectic schedule or disrupted plan has been rescued by the instant solution of the drive-through.

But all that glitters is not gold! This belief that you can have it all now is leading to major heartache for an entire generation. The younger generations have grown up to believe they should have everything now that their parents worked an entire lifetime to earn. So you find couples in their thirties and forties under mountainous debt loads, disillusioned about life, and filled with anger and pain. Our national economy suffers the same fate, and economically uncertain days are made profoundly more frightening by these debt loads.

Still, the *spiritual* fallout from this lie is deadlier than any material frustration. This lie would have us believe that our prayers compel God to work the way we want when we want every time we call on Him. Accordingly, we expect God to work in harmony with our personal timetable. We expect God to respond affirmatively and immediately to our every request. After all, we deserve it all, and we deserve it all *now!*

Lie #3: "If You Have to Wait, Something Is Wrong!"

This third lie is a natural by-product of the first two. Replay your mental tapes on the common experiences of being stuck in traffic, waiting in a long line at the store, having a flight delayed, etc. In every situation, doesn't part of your frustration result from the belief that making someone wait like this is wrong? Making someone wait unexpectedly is wrong, unfair, unjust, immoral! Admit it—don't you feel that way? Don't you find yourself believing that when you are stuck waiting, for any reason, something is wrong?

Think about Brad and Darlene or about anyone you know

who is stuck waiting for resolution to a long-term crisis. Don't you find in them a sense of anger over the injustice they face? Haven't you discovered the same uncomfortable attitude in your own life?

When we are snared by the web of these contemporary deceptions, our ability to trust and/or enjoy the way God works is disastrously affected.

SPIRITUAL FALLOUT

You be the judge. Let your imagination run loose as you place yourself in the following situations. Then take a reading of your spiritual barometer. Do a little honest assessment of your response to circumstances like those below. Ask yourself, "If—or more accurately, when—this happens to me, how do I feel toward the Lord?" See if you don't spot evidence in your life of the spiritual fallout from our "I deserve it now" society.

- You have aggressively and diligently prayed for a long time over a physical need in your life, but God's intervention is nowhere in sight.
- Your company just announced layoffs, and your department is on the list for closure. The weight of the crisis grows exponentially as you get closer to D-day without any firm leads on the future. There is no clue of God's handiwork anywhere in the situation.
- It is decision time—be it financial, career-oriented, medical, etc. But your earnest searching and praying for God's direction gives you no clues about what to do.
- You are the last in your circle of friends who is still single. Internally your desire for a partner in life behaves like a boisterous skeptic who ridicules your trust in God's wisdom. You pray and wait and yearn for God's perfect direction, but you have no prospects and little

remaining energy for a serious relationship. How could God take so long?

- One of your children has become a prodigal. You pray for him or her and try to trust the Lord for him or her, but the wheels of God's deliverance are nowhere to be heard.
- You face a major financial hurdle that appears impossible to overcome. You are depending on the Lord to help you handle it. But with the passing of time the hurdle looms larger and any possible solutions in the past shrink away as wishful thinking.
- Whatever the specific situation, your life hurts, and there is no light at the end of the tunnel. In fact, you can no longer even imagine an end to the tunnel.

During times like these—times when the circumstances of life don't make sense—it is easy for the lies of the world around us to fog our thinking. These lies, fueled by our own impatience and desire for control, spark ferocious conflict over questions about God's timing.

"What's wrong? Why isn't God doing something now? Why does He make me wait? I believe He is faithful and good and that He cares intimately about all my ways, but why is He putting me on hold and making me wait? It doesn't seem right. It's doesn't seem fair. I don't understand. If God is making me wait, something must be wrong."

Does any of this sound familiar? Finding rest when life doesn't make sense can become a gut-wrenching, spiritual battle that threatens the viability of our faith. However, contrary to the pervasive attitude around us, waiting is not necessarily wrong! Periods of waiting can be some of the healthiest, most enlightening, intensive growth experiences through which the Lord takes us. Periods of uncertainty can produce deep roots. And deep roots produce lasting health.

If we learn to wait on the Lord, as opposed to toughing it

out through shaky, self-induced perseverance, we will discover a new depth for our faith and new dimensions of God's rest.

AN INVITATION

If God would repeat His invitation to Brad and Darlene or to any of us in our modern world, He would say something like this.

> You who face the crises and dilemmas of life on this sin-stained planet, I, the Lord of Hosts, now invite to discover what it means to wait on Me. I invite you who live in this stress-packed, frenetically paced, and ulcer-prone world to exchange your anxiety for My peace. I invite you who are weary and heavy-laden to discover My rest at the deepest core of your being.

Be warned! There will be times when trying to wait on the Lord will feel abnormal. You'll feel that you are going upstream against the flow. It may feel like you are trying to take a slow walk down the middle of a rush-hour freeway. Dodge the traffic! Pull over to the side. And give God room to do something radical in your life.

THE BOTTOM LINE

Waiting on the Lord is the timeless answer to our contemporary need for rest in the midst of life's storms.

CHAPTER TWO

Waiting Room Choices

Waiting room experiences . . . No one ever chooses to be stuck in the waiting room. And everyone stuck in the waiting room is preoccupied with one thing—getting out. These experiences can crash upon us suddenly or swagger up slowly. They can catch us by complete surprise or approach in full view. They can arise from any number of circumstances and occur at every stage of life. They don't ask for permission, and they don't leave many options. In fact, in the waiting room there is only one real choice given to us: how we will respond to the waiting.

We cannot choose the circumstances that fall our way, but we do choose our response to them. We may not have everything under control, but no one else controls our response. God may allow a waiting room experience as a tool for our growth, but He does not dictate our response to it. The response of our heart and the attitudes of our will lie solely within the realm of our choice regardless of our circumstances.

You may want to kick or scream or run away, but the Lord says, "Accept the process and find rest in Me." As an individual, a family, or even an entire church, when the Lord puts you in the waiting room, will you fight with Him or lean on Him? In the waiting room, what choice will you make?

Not long ago, a church in Southern California and a pastor 2,000 miles away in the Midwest both found themselves stuck with waiting room choices.

In an enviable facility, located amidst schools and homes and a bustling community, the believers in that church were a healthy body. They offered a unique sense of community against the backdrop of the teeming individualism of a large metropolitan area. Life in the church was good, and the future looked bright—until one day, surprising everyone, the pastor resigned. Prompted by events that have nothing to do with the point of this book, his resignation instantly thrust this family of believers into the grinding search process for a new shepherd.

Caught off-guard, but undaunted, the members of the church began right away to pray together. They sought the guidance of the Spirit as they searched for, contacted, and interviewed men who might serve as the shepherd of their flock. Most of the members knew it would take a while to find the right man; however, none expected the process to drag on for any length of time.

Months crawled by. With each passing month, the draining toll on the church's leadership increased. Some of the members grew frustrated. Many left to find a place where the waiting room was a thing of the past. About the eight or nine month point, the search committee identified one man whom they felt would be an appropriate candidate. They shared their progress with the congregation. They reported on their prayer, their correspondence, their interviews, and their enthusiasm about this candidate.

Encouragement collapsed into despair when this first candidate pulled himself out of contention. Intellectually, they knew if he had been God's man, this wouldn't have happened. And if he wasn't God's man, they should be glad he had withdrawn his name. They tried to convince themselves, "This must be for the best." Nevertheless, the experience was discouraging. The passing of time has a way of dampening robust faith.

Renewed prayer and rebounding enthusiasm carried the day at the one year point when the search committee announced they had a candidate ready to meet the church. His week of meetings and interviews met with positive response. Nearly 90 percent of the congregation voted to call this man as their new pastor.

A full year without a senior pastor is a long haul. Dwindling attendance, eroding finances, and diminished energy for ministry were some of the effects felt by this church during the long year of searching and waiting. Many saw the positive vote to call this pastor as a sign that God was about to end this difficult period. They yearned for it to be over. If you have ever been there, you know what I mean.

But he said no.

Every member of the church felt the blow of his refusal. They were ready. They had been faithful. They had prayed. It looked so positive. The thought of starting over was disheartening. How much longer could God keep them in the waiting room? How could they experience any kind of rest in the midst of so much uncertainty and discouragement? It didn't make sense.

Sure, they could crank up the search committee and trudge along further on this journey. But the real issue facing this church was much tougher. Could they genuinely choose to wait on the Lord? Would they choose to keep trusting God when they were emotionally wiped out? Though they felt horrible, with all thoughts of the future cast back into the wind, would they choose to accept God's timetable as their preference? Could they discover that elusive prize of rest in this uncertain and unending situation?

Nine more grueling, long months passed before another candidate came to meet with this church.

I was that final candidate, and I now serve as pastor of that church. And as amazing as it has been to all of us, my wife and I had gone through an experience almost identical to that of the church. At the very time the church began its search for a new pastor, we began to sense God moving us to consider a new ministry. While the church talked with other men around the country, we were speaking to other churches around the country. While the church saw its enthusiasm rise and fall, we watched our spirits soar and crash again at each new starting point.

Both of us were stuck in the waiting room. Both of us were eager for answers. Both of us wanted the process to be over. Neither of us had any idea that God's resolution to our long delay would eventually bring us together. In spite of our emotional roller coaster, we both discovered that intentionally waiting upon the Lord was always the best choice we could make. We could only find true rest in His able hands.

All of us at the church stand in amazement as we look back from the vantage point of hindsight. It is abundantly clear now that we each had lessons to learn in God's curriculum for our lives.

Those days when we questioned God's wisdom look a little different now. Though we could not see Him at work, our perception had nothing to do with reality. He *was* at work. He was on the throne the whole time. Our prayers were being heard, and His arms were open wide. Although we felt stuck, God was actively at work to unite a pastor and a church at the right time in the right way.

And we discovered the depth and breadth and beauty of Scripture as it addresses those of us in desperate need of His rest.

HEAR HIS OFFER FOR YOURSELF

If you are in the midst of a waiting room experience, allow these verses to shower over you. Read them twice. Read them slowly. Hear the Lord's voice address you at your point of need.

> *"Let the beloved of the LORD rest secure in him, for he shields him all day long, and the one the LORD loves rests between his shoulders."*
>
> (Deuteronomy 33:12)

> *Wait for the LORD; be strong and take heart and wait for the LORD.*
>
> (Psalm 27:14)

> *"In repentance and rest is your salvation, in quietness and trust is your strength, but you would have none of it!" . . . He rises to show you compassion. . . . Blessed are all who wait for him.*
>
> (Isaiah 30:15, 18)

> *Since ancient times, no one has heard, no ear has perceived, no eye has seen any God besides you who acts on behalf of those who wait for him.*
>
> (Isaiah 64:4)

> *My soul finds rest in God alone; my salvation comes from him. He alone is my rock and my salvation; he is my fortress, I will never be shaken. . . . My salvation and my honor depend on God; he is my mighty rock, my refuge. Trust in him at all times, O people; pour out your hearts to him, for God is our refuge.*
>
> (Psalm 62:1-2, 7-8)

Can you feel the promise of these words resonate deep within you? Do you hear them crying out to become a reality in your life? They invite you to discover a way of life that differs greatly from the "normal" twentieth-century experience. They invite you to discover the very source of rest for which you are craving.

WAITING ON THE LORD DEFINED

Up to this point we have talked about the fact that rest can only be cultivated from the inside out. We have identified the Old Testament concept of waiting on the Lord as the key to cultivating the place of rest deep inside. However, we have danced around the phrase without providing a succinct definition. Let's zero in and take a stab at defining what it means to wait on the Lord.

Waiting on the Lord is never a matter of sitting back, folding our arms, and sipping mint juleps on the veranda with a *que sera sera* attitude. It is a position of active dependence on the Lord. Waiting on the Lord is a practical way to describe what it means to live by faith. Waiting on the Lord is what happens when we translate a general desire to trust God into specific practice on a day-to-day level. It is an intentional, aggressive, and active choice of the will. To wait on the Lord means choosing to hold out for His solution, His results, His direction, and His timing—regardless of how long or what direction He takes.

A precise definition of what it means to wait on the Lord might go like this:

Waiting on the Lord means . . .

"To place circumstances, desires, and people into the Lord's hands and rest in His ability to work things out— His way and in His time."

Whether the issues you face deal primarily with circumstances, unsatisfied desires, the important people in your life, or some combination of all three, waiting on the Lord means placing them all in His hands. The Apostle Paul would say, give them away to the Lord through prayer and petition (see Philippians 4:6). Genuine rest happens when, having placed matters in the Lord's hands, you leave them there!

Permit me to be frank. If we are to understand what it means to wait on the Lord, we must be brutally honest about our fierce battle with *time*. The problem is not that we don't trust the Lord or that we don't desire to trust Him. God has convinced us that He is trustworthy and deserving of our faith. Our struggle is that His timing is rarely the same as ours. By its very nature, waiting on the Lord implies a struggle with timing. And because we hate to wait, any delay strains the emotional buoyancy of our faith.

Scripture is full of men and women who testify to the work of God as they waited on Him. Perhaps their example of faith will be an encouragement to you. Perhaps their testimony will remind you that you aren't alone in this struggle. Their experiences with waiting on the Lord will make it clear that your circumstances do not automatically imply God's displeasure. His making you wait does not mean He does not love you or that He has forgotten you!

THE WITNESS OF HISTORY

As we read through the Scriptures, we notice a pattern. Time after time godly men and women who became models of faith found themselves stuck with waiting room choices. For some, this period of waiting was incredibly long. For others, the intensity of their situation more than compensated for its brevity.

Noah: We know his story well. Living where there had

never been rain, far from the shores of the sea, he spent decades building a boat—a primitive Queen Mary, minus amenities. These years were not only decades of obedience but required sustained waiting on the Lord. Noah spent his best years at a job that got no respect, was destined to be terminated, and faced an uncertain future.

Moses: For forty years he lived in exile in the wilderness. For forty years he waited, burdened for his people, with no inkling as to how the Lord would deliver them.

Job: Words can't do justice to Job's commitment to honor the Lord from his perch atop the garbage heap. Although we can quickly read his story and are familiar with its ending, while he sat there day after day scraping his sores he had no word about the future and little help from his friends. Yet, Job still placed his hope for answers and restoration in the Lord's hands.

Hannah: She endured years and years of heckling from her rival, Peninnah. Yet, all the while she entrusted her barrenness into the Lord's hands and waited on Him for deliverance. Samuel was God's answer. The fruit of her waiting was the point man used by God to guide Israel's transition into a kingdom.

Elijah: Day after day, encamped by the brook Kerith, separated from everyone and everything, Elijah learned to wait on the Lord for the necessities of life.

Shadrach, Meshach, and Abednego: Their wait was relatively brief. However, the short time during their arrest, sentencing, and walk to that inferno of an incinerator must have seemed like an eternity of moments. It was a time like we've all had, when every step gives rise to new battles with doubt and fear. Time grinds into slow motion, while relentless waves of emotion rise and fall. Yet, they entrusted their physical and spiritual well-being into the hands of the Lord; and they displayed a rest so deep that it produced circumstances that caused their guards to lose their lives.

Elizabeth: She and her husband Zechariah were "upright in the sight of God" (Luke 1:6), but she was plagued by the curse of barrenness. And as if the suffering of childlessness weren't enough, in her day people believed childlessness to be a sign of God's judgment. However, she lived obediently, entrusting herself and her situation to the Lord. God's resolution to her long wait? She became the mother of the one who would pave the way for the Messiah—John the Baptist.

AN HONEST PICTURE OF WAITING ROOM EMOTIONS

Don't get me wrong. The process of waiting on the Lord is no nifty experience of bliss and tranquillity. It does not mean parking your emotions and enjoying beautiful sunsets while God miraculously works out the details in order to fulfill your personal wants. Situations that call for waiting on the Lord are often intense, demanding dilemmas. They are times when we find ourselves stretched to the limit. There are no magic formulas. Prepackaged formulas do not work in the minefields of life.

God has preserved a brutally honest picture of this process in Psalm 13. In this Psalm, David gives us an intimate glimpse into the tug-of-war between his spirit, his emotions, his will, and his faith as he waited on the Lord. He also allows us to peek at the key to his victory. His cries ring true in each of us as we recall similar times and similar struggles.

> *How long, O LORD? Will you forget me forever?*
> *How long will you hide your face from me?*
> *How long must I wrestle with my thoughts and*
>   *every day have sorrow in my heart?*
> *How long will my enemy triumph over me?*

> *Look on me and answer, O LORD my God.*
>> *Give light to my eyes or I will sleep in death;*
> *my enemy will say, "I have overcome him,"*
>> *and my foes will rejoice when I fall.*
>
> *But*
>
> *I trust in your unfailing love;*
>> *my heart rejoices in your salvation.*
> *I will sing to the LORD,*
>> *for he has been good to me.*

Can you hear the ligaments of David's faith stretch to the breaking point? Here the man after God's own heart is praying with such audacity, such savage honesty that we feel uncomfortable. These are the agonizing cries of a man in the waiting room. We would cringe at such words if spoken in our church services. David feels forgotten and cut off from God. "Lord, I can't stand it any longer. I am so far from rest, I may not survive. If You don't give me a little light—a reason for hope—I may not live through this!"

However, Psalm 13 does not end hopelessly mired in struggle. It ends in hope and praise. Why?

Take a close look. The key to the change in David's perspective was his willful choice to trust in God's unfailing love. He deliberately redirected his attention and chose to dwell on the character and word of his God. And that changed his outlook. When he turned his focus away from his circumstances and onto his Lord, hope and praise and even singing resulted. Only a heart at authentic rest can sing and praise.

In the waiting room, *you* choose your response. Only *you* decide where your focus will be. You can choose to focus on your circumstances—this comes naturally—or on your God. You may be stuck waiting in circumstances beyond your control, but how you wait and on whom you rest is a choice you make for yourself.

Wait on the Lord because your ways and your resources will never compare with His. Wait on the Lord because you know His timing is impeccable and always for your best and His glory. Place your circumstances, desires, and people into the Lord's hands, and rest in His ability to work things out—in His way and in His time. As you do this, you'll give Him a free hand to create a calm center in your life, a place from which genuine rest can flow. It's your choice.

THE BOTTOM LINE

"Stand at the crossroads and look; ask for the ancient paths, ask where the good way is, and walk in it, and you will find rest for your souls!"

(Jeremiah 6:16)

CHAPTER THREE

Facing a Crisis

The news was bad. No, that is too mild. It was absolutely horrendous. It was the stuff of which nightmares are made, only this was real life—all too real. Who would have thought it could happen now, today, or that it would be so bad? His mind blurred as those familiar questions began to race. Questions like, "How will I tell everyone?" "How will they react?" "What should I do first?" "Why didn't I see it coming?" "Surely I could have prevented it somehow." "What will everyone think of me?" "I'm not sure I have the strength to face this, but who can I call?" "Where should I turn?"

None of us will go very long without running headfirst into some type of crisis. You can't plan for them, but you know that now and then you will run into them. Or should I say, they will run into you. When it happens, how will you respond?

It is during times of crisis that our calm center—our place of rest and faith—is stretched to the limit. Perhaps that is why the man we are about to meet is such a good model of what it means to wait on the Lord. The way he handled a major crisis gives us an opportunity to observe how we might wait on the Lord when we find ourselves in a crisis situation. The man I am writing about is one you may know. God recorded his crisis and his response for all time in the pages of Scripture.

His name is Jehoshaphat. He was one of those Old Testament kings whose record stands out among story after story of fickle characters who led the people of God astray. Jehoshaphat had a life and influence that shone in contrast with the murky records of many other Jewish kings. Don't misunderstand me—Jehoshaphat was not perfect. He had moments of brilliance, but he also had moments of great failure. In general he devoted himself to following the Lord and "walked in the ways his father David had followed" (2 Chronicles 17:3). But upon close scrutiny you will also find the trail of his life strewn with painful blunders along the way.

Precisely because he wasn't perfect, he makes a great example for us to study. If he were perfect, it might be tempting to gloss over his example on the assumption we could never do what he did. He was a man like us who made progress one surge at a time. Just like us, he often took two steps forward and one step back.

Yet, during his life he learned that the best plan of action is always to put matters into the Lord's hands. He learned that after you entrust a situation to the Lord, you wait for Him to work things out in His way and in His time. The lessons he learned prepared him to face the engulfing crisis at hand. His example, recorded in 2 Chronicles 20, is so significant that we will camp there for two chapters. I want us to linger over the details and nuances of his actions, so that we might carefully observe the depth of his rest in the face of a national crisis.

THE CRISIS UNFOLDS

Second Chronicles 20 opens with these words:

*After this, the Moabites and Ammonites with some of the
Meunites came to make war on Jehoshaphat.*

These names of neighboring nations may not mean a whole lot to you; so let's try to put them into perspective. If you can visualize where the Dead Sea is in the land of Israel, you know enough geography to understand what was taking place. Imagine drawing a large clock around the Dead Sea, with the center of the clock in the center of the Dead Sea. Now sweep clockwise from 8 o'clock up to 12 o'clock and you've got the nation of Judah pegged. This kingdom of Judah is where Jehoshaphat reigned as king. Take your clock again and continue sweeping from about 1 o'clock down to 6 o'clock. Now you understand the homeland of these enemies.

Let's try it another way. If Wisconsin were the nation of Israel, then the first verse of 2 Chronicles 20 would read: "After this, the Michiganites and those from Indiana came around the bottom of Lake Michigan to make war on Wisconsin."

No matter how you slice it, the news is that the neighboring nations are on the warpath against Jehoshaphat and against the nation of Judah. The people of God will soon be under attack. Verse 2 allows us to eavesdrop on the message just as Jehoshaphat heard it spoken:

*Some men came and told Jehoshaphat, "A vast army is
coming against you from Edom, from the other side of the
Sea. It is already in Hazazon Tamar (that is, En Gedi)"*
[i.e., at O'Hare airport, in our midwestern U.S. scenario].

It is at this point that we begin to see things unfold from Jehoshaphat's perspective. With these words we hear what Jehoshaphat heard about the size and location of this attacking enemy. Keep in mind that until these messengers arrived at the palace, Jehoshaphat and his advisers had no idea of the advancing army.

Although it is easy to lose this in the English translation, the description of this army in the Hebrew tells us something crucial if we are to grasp the urgency of this crisis. The words "vast army" could be translated "a great host," "an awesome horde," "a ready-for-battle, fired-up, angry army." There is the strong sense in the original language of a noisy or rowdy crowd. It is the kind of word you would use to describe a riotous mob.

You might find this kind of attitude in a high school locker room after the coach has given his football team their pre-game pep talk. Even if you've never played football, you have witnessed this kind of locker-room scene on television or in the movies. As the coach finishes his speech, the team's enthusiasm erupts with screaming and yelling. The players begin hitting lockers. They begin hitting one another in their excitement over the ensuing battle. Adrenaline flows at breakneck speed because they are confident this battle will be theirs for the taking. Multiply the size of that football team along with that emotion and aggression a few thousand times, and you may begin to grasp the intensity of this awesome horde that has come down to make war against Jehoshaphat.

Put yourself in his shoes for a moment. You have just learned you will soon be attacked. You have learned that your neighbors have formed an allegiance to wipe you out. The size and the aggressiveness of their army is immense. And to put the last piece of straw on the camel's back, you learn one more fact: this mob-like army is only fifteen hours away by foot! En Gedi was merely fifteen hours south of Jerusalem (according to C.F. Keil and F. Delitzsch, *Commentary on the Old Testament: The Second Book of Chronicles*, page 386). When translated into battle plans, this means that you could find yourself under attack in Jerusalem at almost any time.

Jehoshaphat's crisis was immediate. Both personally and nationally, it was filled with frightening implications. This was a life or death matter, no doubt about it. In every respect it carried all the dynamics of the worst crises we will ever face. As a

result, his response to this situation is not only inspirational—
it is instructional.

His response was not a magic formula. Real life does not
occur in tidy little packages. Yet, Jehoshaphat faced six critical
junctures in this crisis. Six crucial points in which he had to
deliberately choose the path he would follow. Six moments of
decision that would contribute to or detract from his ability to
experience rest. His action at each juncture provides us with a
model to be followed.

JUNCTURE #1: WHEN CONFRONTED
BY A CRISIS ... COMMIT YOUR WILL TO
SEEK THE LORD

Waiting on the Lord is a deliberate choice. As David demonstrated
in Psalm 13, it means willfully redirecting your focus onto the
Lord instead of fixating on the problem. It means resting in His
infinite ability, not on your own limited resources. Waiting on the
Lord refers to the posture of your life expressed in both an attitude
of the heart and a commitment of the will to seek Him. In the
response of Jehoshaphat to the news of the impending invasion,
you can clearly see the public and private impact of his decision.

> *Alarmed, Jehoshaphat resolved to inquire of the LORD, and*
> *he proclaimed a fast for all Judah. The people of Judah*
> *came together to seek help from the LORD; indeed, they*
> *came from every town in Judah to seek him.*

> (2 Chronicles 20:3-4)

Break this down with me. "Jehoshaphat resolved to inquire
of the LORD." Literally this verse says, "He set his face to seek
the Lord." This was the firm resolve of a man who had charted
a path from which he would not turn back. This is that setting

of the jaw that conveys unswerving conviction. "Don't bother me with alternatives—this is the way we are going. No argument." The focus of the king's attention was solely on the Lord.

Having chosen his path, he then called the entire country to join him by fasting. Reading these words today seems so matter-of-fact. So sanitary. So spiritual. We can read ahead so quickly that his actions sound completely tame. Simple. Predictable. Ah, don't be fooled! This call to fast is no mere religious exercise.

If you recall, they had no TV, no daily newspaper, no radio, and no emergency broadcast network in the event of a local disaster. The only way to proclaim a national fast was to send riders throughout the land to inform the people. This took time! But the riders were only the first part. Jehoshaphat also gave people time to journey from "every town in Judah." Some of those towns were further away than the enemy! He was so committed to wait on the Lord, to place this battle in the Lord's hands, that he refused to regard the extra time needed for people to join him in Jerusalem as a problem. Why would the king do things this way?

His course of action was not just instinctive. It was a definite choice to wait on the Lord in this manner. Not too many years earlier, in order to intimidate potential enemies, Jehoshaphat had allied himself with Ahab. Ahab, as you may recall, was the godless, ruthless, apostate ruler of the northern kingdom, Israel. (This description might be too favorable.) Political alliances of the type made with Ahab were made to insure greater protection in time of war; but they were forbidden by God. Jehoshaphat's course of action was decidedly different this go-around. This time he made a deliberate choice to wait upon the Lord.

Jehoshaphat's choice to handle this matter differently than before was not motivated by his nation's military weakness either. If that were the problem, we who read of his situation today might be tempted to write off his response as a typical foxhole prayer vigil. The fact of the matter is, Jehoshaphat and the nation of

Judah were very powerful at that time. Second Chronicles 17 tells us that the size of his army numbered 1,160,000 "experienced fighting men" (vv. 13-18). His prayer was not motivated by the terror of weakness. They were not inferior to their enemies.

Jehoshaphat was motivated by the conviction that God's way, God's timing, and God's ability were all greater than anything he could do alone. His response demonstrates the transforming power of rest that flows out of the calm center of a person who trusts the Lord. He chose to honor God by waiting, as opposed to taking matters into his own hands and his own strength. He had learned the meaning of the words spoken by the prophet to his father:

> "The eyes of the Lord range throughout the earth to
> strengthen those whose hearts are fully committed to him."
>
> (2 Chronicles 16:9)

If we are going to learn what it is to wait on the Lord, we must take note of those actions that go against our normal nature. For myself, when confronted by a crisis like this I know my own tendencies. If I had been Jehoshaphat my natural reaction would have been to send riders out to gather my army. Having gathered the army, I might have had us pray for a moment somewhere along the way in the process, but it wouldn't have been my first thought. I may have even asked others to pray for us as we charged toward the enemy. But I probably would have been well down the road, having long since committed myself to a course of action dependent on my own strength, before I would have thought to stop and pray. At that point, I'd be asking God to bless what I had already decided to do.

What about you? Can you see the radical approach Jehoshaphat took? Can you feel the depth of his commitment to wait on the Lord? Can you hear the trust in his voice? Can you picture the clear conviction in his eyes? Is his response different than yours would have been?

Our journey of learning to wait on the Lord in the face of a crisis begins with this lesson of the will. Willfully choosing to seek the Lord is an act of obedience that ignites faith at the core of our lives.

JUNCTURE #2: WHEN YOU PRAY . . . FOCUS ON THE LORD, NOT ON THE PROBLEM

"From every town in Judah" the people came. Apprehensive perhaps. Tired and hungry perhaps. Some undoubtedly excited by the bold faith of their king. Some certainly fearful of the unknown ahead of them. Some were just curious. And some were convinced this was a definite appointment with disaster. Did any arrive with a clear idea of what was to come? I doubt it.

Try to imagine some of the conversations that took place as these people gathered at the temple. Rumors about the size and fierceness of the attacking army would be enough to frighten the strongest of warriors. The skeptics—always prepared with a cynical word—would eagerly tout their better ideas about handling this crisis. The buzz of the crowd was nearly deafening.

Suddenly it all changed. In an instant the noise of the crowd turned to silence—that painful, absolute silence of fear, anticipation, and curiosity all rolled into one. It was as if everyone held their breath simultaneously. Why the change? Out into the sunlight stepped their king. Under the heat of the sun and the scorching scrutiny of this assembled mob, Jehoshaphat would have the words to direct them. His words, however, were not addressed to his people. His words were to his God.

Jehoshaphat's prayer is a model of how to pray in faith. Of

how to pray in dependence on our God. Of how to express our commitment to wait on the Lord as we speak to Him. Of the kind of prayer that strengthens rest and puts distress into perspective. Jehoshaphat taught us to pray in a way that focuses on the Lord, not on the problem. When you think of all they faced at that moment, it is astounding to notice that of the four main sections in Jehoshaphat's prayer, only one specifically described the problem at hand. Only one!

First, He Reviewed God's Incredible Power

> *"O Lord . . . are you not the God who is in heaven?*
> *You rule over all the kingdoms of the nations.*
> *Power and might are in your hand, and no one can*
> *withstand you."*

(2 Chronicles 20:6)

Standing there before the people of his country, knowing that at any moment they would face a mighty enemy, Jehoshaphat honored the Lord. He reviewed the fact that regardless of the strength of his enemies, God was stronger. His prayer was consumed by a focus on the sufficiency of his God, and he led his people toward that same preoccupation.

Second, He Recalled God's Faithfulness

> *"Our God, did you not drive out the inhabitants of this*
> *land before your people Israel? . . . we will stand in your*
> *presence . . . and will cry out to you in our distress, and you*
> *will hear us and save us."*

(2 Chronicles 20:7-9)

The same God whose power is unequaled in all the universe is our God. And He has consistently demonstrated His faithfulness. God's faithfulness in the past provides the tangible impetus to approach the current situation with fresh faith.

Third, He Now Turned to the Problem at Hand

> *"But now here are men of Ammon, Moab and*
> *Mount Seir . . . they are repaying us by coming to drive us*
> *out of the possession you gave us as an inheritance."*

(2 Chronicles 20:10-11)

That's all he said about the problem itself! "Hey, Jehoshaphat, you've got God's attention—don't shortchange the problem. Don't be a wimp. Tell Him what's going on. Tell Him how scared we are."

When you think about the intensity of their crisis, this simple description seems rather anemic. However, because his focus was not on the problem but on the Lord, little detail was necessary. Our God knows all of our circumstances and knows every detail about the dilemmas we face. He is not dependent on us for information. Jehoshaphat knew that! Why is it that we often feel compelled to elaborate every nuance of a problem when we pray? Perhaps it is time to learn a greater degree of rest in the midst of our prayer. Prayer that leads to rest firmly recognizes that God knows the details better than we do.

Fourth and Finally, He Declared Simple but Absolute Dependence on the Lord

> *"We do not know what to do, but our eyes are on you."*

(2 Chronicles 20:12)

This kind of confident, willing to wait, absolutely dependent prayer sounds quite different from what I suspect most of our own "panic prayers" sound like. We tend to place our eyes on the size of our mountain rather than on the One who moves mountains. We become overwhelmed by our own insufficiency instead of His sufficiency. Instead of focusing on God's power, we focus on our own weakness. Instead of focusing on our God, it is easy to become transfixed on every facet of our problem and every reason for fear.

The very way we pray often increases the level of our fear instead of the depth of our faith!

We can learn from Jehoshaphat. Obviously prayer is a key to genuine rest; but we need to practice the kind of prayer that focuses on the Lord, not the problem. As Isaiah wrote, "Lift your eyes and look to the heavens" (40:26). Prayer that energizes rest naturally flows out of a commitment to seek the Lord. It requires turning your eyes toward Him. And this kind of prayer leads naturally into a willingness to wait.

JUNCTURE #3: AFTER YOU HAVE PRAYED . . . BE WILLING TO WAIT

Thousands responded to the king's call to prayer and fasting. They gathered from all corners of the country. They listened attentively as their king prayed earnestly. In face after face you could sense prayer and agreement as the king prayed to the God of their fathers. You could see mouths moving in unison as the king spoke his final words: "We do not know what to do, but our eyes are upon you."

Now what?

Having fasted and prayed, what do we do next?

With penetrating certainty and profound silence verse 13 screams out loudly to us:

All the men of Judah, with their wives and children and little ones, stood there *before the LORD. (emphasis added)*

Did you see that? They just "stood there." Waiting. The entire crowd stood as one man, waiting on the Lord, totally dependent on Him. Paint the picture carefully so that you don't miss any of it. There they were standing and waiting. How long did they wait? How long were they planning to stand there? Were children starting to squirm? Were stomachs beginning to growl? How were they expecting God to answer their prayer? It appears as if they were willing to wait on the Lord as long as it took and were willing to accept whatever form in which He chose to answer.

I can't help but wonder if sitting off to one side, probably on a porch in the shade, you could find the skeptics. Can you see them there watching? Snickering? Now and then speaking to one another? After a few moments of stillness the waiting probably got to them so much, they couldn't keep silent any longer. You can almost hear their hoots and catcalls.

"Okay, you prayed. Now what are you waiting for?"

"Hey, King, that army's gonna be here any minute. Do you plan to stand here until they invade or what?"

"Yo, doesn't God help those who help themselves?"

"Are you a man or a mouse?"

"Let's go—we're not afraid to fight these guys."

"C'mon, be sensible. Would God have given us swords if He hadn't intended for us to use them?"

"Faith is nice, but when are you going to get practical?"

"Aren't you being a little fanatical about this religious stuff?"

There are always skeptics. And silence is always painful. Yet, is it not possible that prayer is the most tangible and practical thing we can do in the face of a crisis? Waiting on the Lord grows first of all from a decision to seek His face. It leads naturally to concentrated and dependent prayer. And prayer energizes our willingness to wait. Taken all together this

approach fuels our ability to experience rest in spite of the crisis we face.

But what are we to do when it is time to take action?

THE BOTTOM LINE

Contrary to popular opinion, prayer is the most tangible
and practical thing we can do in the face of a crisis.

CHAPTER FOUR

Near the Edge of the Cliff

Edge of the cliff experiences . . . Jehoshaphat was in for one. We've all had them. Times when circumstances carry us inevitably toward the valley of despair. Times when we know we'll soon be standing on the edge of the cliff and yet we have no idea what the valley below holds in store. Quite often, the worst moments of such experiences are those just before we actually reach the cliff. The moments when our imagination runs out of control. The moments when we have a vague idea of what might lie ahead, but have absolutely no idea how it will be resolved.

Back to the example of Jehoshaphat. At each juncture to this point we have seen that he chose to keep waiting on the Lord in practical ways. When confronted with the bad news, he made a commitment of his will to seek the Lord. When it was time to pray, he focused on the Lord, not the problem. After he had prayed, he waited for direction. Now it was time to move forward, to head toward the cliff.

How could he move forward and yet remain at rest? How

could he lead his people directly toward the enemy and have any hope they might still wait on the Lord in their hearts?

JUNCTURE #4: WHEN IT IS TIME TO ACT ... DELIBERATELY REVIEW THE CHARACTER OF GOD

Having set his face to seek the Lord, having prayed, and having waited before the Lord, Jehoshaphat now received an answer from the Lord through the prophet Jahaziel.

> *"Do not be afraid or discouraged because of this vast army. For the battle is not yours, but God's. Tomorrow march down against them. They will be climbing up by the Pass of Ziz. . . . You will not have to fight this battle. Take up your positions; stand firm and see the deliverance the Lord will give you, O Judah and Jerusalem."*

(2 Chronicles 20:15-17)

What a tremendous answer and encouragement from the Lord. The people of Judah were so overwhelmed that, led by their king, they all fell down in worship before the Lord. They began to praise "the LORD, the God of Israel, with a very loud voice" (2 Chronicles 20:19). I imagine this was one of those once-in-a-lifetime, completely overpowering experiences. One of those moments when every fiber in our bodies explodes with adoration and praise to the Lord who "acts on behalf of those who wait for him" (Isaiah 64:4).

But hold on. Yes, the words of the prophet were like music to the ears. Indeed, God had heard and had answered. But when you look carefully, you'll see there were still many unanswered, disconcerting questions. When the initial euphoria of worship fades, the agony of the unanswered returns. Sure, the prophet said God would fight for them. But he also said they would find the enemy climbing up the pass toward them. An army that is actively advancing does not sound like a subdued foe! And why did the prophet say, "Take up your positions"? That would only be necessary if there was going to be a battle. How exactly was God going to fight this battle for them? They may have thought, "If God would only tell us how things are going to be worked out, being calm would be a whole lot easier." Sound familiar?

At precisely this point we learn another crucial lesson about waiting on the Lord. When it is time to act, we should deliberately review God's character. And this is exactly what the people did the next day. In spite of many unknown details regarding God's plan to accomplish His promise, this mighty parade of people marched to the scene of the battle with assurance. Our ability to rest in confidence is directly linked to our understanding of God's character.

You may be thinking, "How can we be so sure they were confident?" Simple. Actions speak louder than words. Jehoshaphat stood before the people early the next morning and appointed "men to sing to the LORD and to praise him for the splendor of his holiness as they went out at the head of the army."

Singers and musicians were placed at the front! They created a mobile worship service, and their songs caused the people to review and celebrate the trustworthy character of our God. "The splendor of his holiness" is how Jehoshaphat stated it (2 Chronicles 20:21).

Singers in the front. What a wild idea! Can you imagine serving in an army on its way to battle with musicians at the front announcing your arrival? Not only would the enemy be well warned of your advance, but your musicians are usually not front-line fighting men. Being a football fan I find it easy to draw a gridiron analogy here.

In many parts of the country you find intense, emotional rivalries between two football teams. One such rivalry is between the Chicago Bears and the Green Bay Packers. Whenever these two teams meet to play, you know fur will fly. Tempers flare, coaches scream, and fans go wild. (If the weather's bad, so much the better!) Jehoshaphat's strategy was equivalent to the Bears' head coach asking me to play on their kickoff return team against Green Bay.

In case you aren't fully aware, on the kickoff twenty-two rather large specimens of humanity line up on opposite sides of the field. With fearless looks of cold-blooded fury, they take a running start and plow full-speed into one another. This is certainly the most dangerous portion of the game. Please understand—I love football. I love to play, and I love to watch. But I also value my life. If I were to go onto the field without extensive training and conditioning—not to mention better size—I would simply be destroyed by those guys. I think the operative word in that case would be "squashed," or maybe "decimated."

Jehoshaphat appointed singers and musicians to lead the "kickoff return team" as they marched toward enemy territory. This was a strategic move, not a symbolic one. Their songs were a deliberate means of helping the people review God's trustworthy character. Without this music their thoughts would have focused on potential bad-news scenarios at the scene of battle. However, instead of panic, their march was filled with praise. Instead of being consumed by what could go wrong, they were transformed by the power of worship.

Even though they were taking action themselves, because of their focus they continued to wait on the Lord for the deliverance He would give. Instead of distress, they marched forward with a tangible sense of rest. When it is time to act, don't sacrifice rest and peace by turning your dependence onto yourself.

Rather, move ahead with deliberate focus on God's character—
"the splendor of his holiness."

What can we learn from the lesson of Jehoshaphat? When
you are nearing the cliff, expand the time you spend in worship.
Dwell in God's presence. Stand beneath the shower of His gaze.
Focus on His character.

Pragmatically, there are many ways to do that. Give yourself
wholeheartedly to the worship experiences designed by your
local church. Attendance on auto-pilot just won't cut it. You
might also invest in or borrow some of the good worship tapes
that are available. Worship through excellent music touches
chords deep within us. Jehoshaphat understood that. My personal recommendation is that you sing out loud along with your
favorite worship tapes. Even if it means hiding in the car, sing
your heart out. Worship is participation. You might also want to
involve yourself in extended times of prayer and Bible study
with other supportive believers.

JUNCTURE #5: AS YOU NEAR THE EDGE OF THE CLIFF . . . BRACE YOURSELF FOR FEAR

Read quickly and you'll miss it. Linger over the words, place
yourself in their shoes, imagine what they were feeling, and perhaps you'll hear the tempest bubbling. Jehoshaphat sensed it.
And wisely, he did something about it.

> *Early in the morning they left for the Desert of Tekoa*
> *[twelve miles to the south]. As they set out, Jehoshaphat*
> *stood and said, "Listen to me, Judah and people of*
> *Jerusalem! Have faith in the LORD your God and you will*
> *be upheld; have faith in his prophets and you will be*
> *successful." After consulting the people [they set out].*

(2 Chronicles 20:20-21)

Granted, this is part of what led to the appointment of singers at the head of the parade, but it illustrates another important juncture in the waiting process. Ask yourself, why did Jehoshaphat stop their progress and stand before them to speak on that morning? Why was he compelled to challenge them to be strong in their faith? Why did he specifically address the outcome of their endeavor? And what exactly what was he "consulting" the people about?

When you move closer to the moment of truth—nearer to the edge of the cliff—invariably your fear quotient multiplies. As a confrontation, decision, deadline, or crisis draws close, fear over the unknown rises. On that morning, as the people of Judah set out, they were heading toward the valley of the unknown. They were actively moving toward the cliff, and it was unsettling to say the least. On a feeling level things were quite different today than yesterday.

Yesterday was a day of answered prayer.
But today is a day of new requests.

Yesterday meant celebration in safety.
But today is a day of real-world threats.

Yesterday we stood before the Lord.
But today we must stand in the battlefield.

Yesterday was a day of beautiful worship.
But today the luster of yesterday is fading.

Yesterday was a day of promises given.
But today is a day for testing those promises.

Yesterday we stood in familiar territory.
But today we walk toward the unknown.

Yesterday today was still tomorrow.
But today there is no turning back,
no bargaining with the clock.

Yesterday was filled with optimism.
But today is filled with questions that ask, "What if?"

Yesterday.
Yesterday it seemed so simple, so clear, so certain.

But that was yesterday.
This is today.

And today my faith seems so weak.
Today my fears are strong.

It always happens that way. The closer you get to the cliff, the more your feelings of faith are muffled by fear. However, don't be too hard on yourself. This makes sense, really. Even though the cliff is rapidly approaching, you still cannot see what God is doing. You cannot see far enough ahead to know how or when God's answer will become reality. Fear of the unknown is normal; when the unknown is charging upon you like a runaway train, fear should be expected.

In moments like these, when the feeling level of your faith falters, you need to remember an important principle: *your faith is not equivalent to your feelings!* Faith and feelings are often companions, but they are vastly different. Faith is what prompts your actions; feelings follow along. Faith is a matter of willful choices; feelings are often involuntary responses. Faith can exist and chart a course of action even when feelings run contrary. You can keep waiting on the Lord, even walking toward the unknown, in spite of what you feel. Faith makes it happen.

Setting out from the walls of safety, Jehoshaphat helped his people brace themselves for the fear they would face. He enabled them to continue waiting on the Lord as they moved forward. He helped them face the unknown by focusing on the known character of God. He laid the groundwork for rest when uncertainty was the only known commodity.

Although they could not see God's hand working ahead of them, He was in fact at work. Although they must have experienced waves of panic as they walked, unknown to them victory had already been obtained.

> *As they began to sing and praise, the Lord set ambushes against the men of Ammon and Moab and Mount Seir . . . they helped to destroy one another. When the men of Judah came to the place that overlooks the desert and looked toward the vast army, they saw only dead bodies lying on the ground; no one had escaped.*

(2 Chronicles 20:22-24)

Can you imagine it? Moments before God's people looked into that valley, their anxiety must have been thick enough to cut with a knife. Those last few steps were probably made with feet that felt like lead. Mouths were silenced by the dry, sticky taste of fear. Eyes that were eager to see for themselves at the same time hoped for an excuse to hide. It was the moment of truth.

Yes, they were people who had waited on the Lord. Yes, they had marched forward by faith. But they were people like us! And none of us looks over the edge of the cliff without thinking twice.

When you wait on the Lord to do what you cannot do, you discover just how much He can do. And, boy, did they find that to be true. With eyes as big as saucers they surveyed the scene, only to discover the battle was already history. God could have resolved it in any number of ways. He was not obligated to do it this way. By waiting on the Lord, they gave Him complete freedom to do whatever He wanted. They found their rest in His character completely apart from and long before they knew His methods. They entrusted their situation into His hands and saw Him work things out in His way and in His perfect timing.

Brace yourself for times of intense fear. Realize that you can continue to move forward by faith in spite of your feelings. Faith is not the absence of fear. Faith is the willingness to follow where God leads regardless of how we feel. Faith is focused on God, "who acts on behalf of those who wait for him" (Isaiah 64:4).

JUNCTURE #6: WHEN IT'S ALL OVER . . . RETURN PRAISE AND HONOR TO THE LORD

Learning to wait on the Lord through the ins and outs of life means not only learning what to do before a crisis, but also learning how to honor the Lord after it is over. Jehoshaphat and his people provide an excellent example of returning praise to the Lord for all He has done. After three days of collecting the plunder God gave them, this is what happened:

> *On the fourth day they assembled in the Valley of Beracah,*
> *where they praised the LORD. . . . Then, led by Jehoshaphat,*
> *all the men of Judah and Jerusalem returned joyfully to*
> *Jerusalem. . . . They entered Jerusalem and went to the*
> *temple of the LORD with harps and lutes and trumpets.*

(2 Chronicles 20:26-28)

They Took Time to Worship the Lord

Right there on the spot, after three days of gathering up the loot, they put a halt to their work and spent time praising the Lord. At this moment of blessing there was no misplaced admiration, no inappropriate credit given to men. Men and women did not lift Jehoshaphat onto their shoulders to parade him around the battlefield. Just as their faces were set on seeking the Lord at the beginning, they now continued to be focused on Him. They took time to recognize all He had done.

Having steadfastly sought the Lord at each step of the crisis, they could do no less than celebrate with Him at the conclusion of it all. There was jubilation of the richest variety right there on the battlefield.

But their jubilation and worship were not limited to the battlefield. Back home were friends and family members who had also fasted and prayed and waited. They needed to participate in this celebration too. The crisis was known publicly, and it was prayed for publicly. Therefore, God's deliverance and resolution were celebrated publicly. So "they entered Jerusalem and went to the temple of the LORD with harps and lutes and trumpets." When God demonstrates His faithfulness to us, it is healthy to publicly proclaim His praises.

How often have you been encouraged by hearing what God has done in the life of a friend? How much has your ability to rest been strengthened by learning of ways God cared for others in similar situations? It not only honors the Lord to give Him public credit, but this also invigorates others. When God works in your life, whether in public or in private, take the time to give Him credit before others. Learn not only to share needs for prayer, but also to share results—God's answers. Taking time for reflection and celebration will deepen the freshness of your faith and your ability to rest. And it will do the same for those around you.

They Created a Permanent Reminder of What God Had Done

Jehoshaphat and his people did more than give verbal praise—they created a permanent reminder of God's work on that day.

On the fourth day they assembled in the Valley of Beracah, where they praised the LORD. That is why it is called the Valley of Beracah.

(2 Chronicles 20:26)

If you are like me, you have probably driven past hundreds of historical markers placed along the roadsides of America. Like me, you rarely think twice about what you might be missing. Jehoshaphat did far more than create a sign and a plaque to identify a site of historical significance. Lest anyone *ever* forget what the Lord had done, they permanently changed the name of the valley to "The Valley of Praise" ("Beracah" means praise). For all time every person who looked at a map, every person who asked for directions, every traveler who passed through this region would be reminded that the Lord had worked a wonder in this place.

Throughout the Scriptures, there is a strong theology of remembrance. God knows that we tend to pray in specific and remember in generalities. We dissect every nuance of a crisis with a fine-tooth comb and recite it in nerve-wracking detail to the Lord. Yet, His mighty acts and faithful works in the past are glossed over with a broad brush. If we haven't kept track of the times and places when God worked in the past, we cannot be encouraged by those memories when our faith is floundering. Our confidence in God in the present is always enhanced by recalling His faithfulness in the past.

On the practical side, you may not have the privilege of renaming a valley or a city or even the street on which you live. So a few simple ideas might be helpful. If you have never started, try keeping a journal of answered prayer. Perhaps you used to be in the practice of keeping a prayer journal, but you have slipped out of the habit. This may be an ideal time to begin your journal again.

Another suggestion would be to set aside one or two holidays a year as special times to review all that God has done recently. Your family photo album, with the addition of short descriptions about the pictured events, can be an inspirational reminder of God's handiwork. Your creativity is the only limit to the number of ways to create permanent memories of what God has done. Once established, those memories will become instigators of praise and worship over and over again.

As you read 2 Chronicles 20, the tone of the chapter is one of calm assurance. But don't sell short the urgency of the people's dilemma. The confident, victorious tone of this passage is a reflection of the way they waited on the Lord. Not only did Jehoshaphat demonstrate the wellspring of rest that is possible in a crisis, but he gave us a living example of how we can discover the same depth of rest for ourselves.

THE BOTTOM LINE

When you wait on the Lord for what you cannot do, you discover just how much He can do!

CHAPTER FIVE

Peace: It's a Question of Ownership

When life is topsy-turvy, when your stomach's churning within resembles the storm brewing without, when circumstances are beyond your control, when anxiety has long since become an old friend, your cry is for peace. If you were given a choice, you would try to escape, to run away. But that choice is rarely an actual option.

Sadly, many choose the escape route anyway. People seek relief from their turmoil by medicating their troubles with chemicals, burying their heads in the sand through overwork, or accepting the diversions of illicit relationships. But when they return to reality, nothing has changed. The same storms still thunder around them, the same pressures still bear down upon them, the same uncertainties still loom before them, and the same acids still boil within them. A brief journey down the false trail of escape does little to create needed internal rest. Instead of relief, escape and denial often make matters worse.

When life is beyond our control and the circumstances bearing down upon us call for panic, what we need is *peace*—a calm center to provide balance and strength in spite of the daily barrage. While we may cry out for a miraculous change in our circumstances, what we truly need is a miraculous change within. We long for a calm center inside to replace the turmoil of our stress. We long for the peace of Christ that passes all understanding.

On a quiet evening, on a familiar lake, a few friends tasted the entire spectrum of emotion and anxiety each of us experiences when circumstances get out of hand. However, what's more important is that in the process they also discovered the key to peace.

A THREE-HOUR CRUISE

They had been so busy during the day that an evening boat ride across the lake sounded like the perfect idea. Away from the crowds, away from incessant demands, there was something therapeutic about an evening on the water. Warm, gentle breezes tumbled off the hillside. Fish performed their sunset dance against the surface of the water. Even the physical demand of working the sails and oars had a rhythmic way of calming their spirits. Each man settled into his own private retreat as they pulled away from shore.

The rougher than normal waters that evening were nothing to cause alarm, though they did require harder than normal work. As hard work is often made more pleasant by cheerful conversation, the scene in the boat soon became one of storytelling and laughter as they muscled their way through the choppy waters. After all, the evening was still young, the company sweet, and the serenity of the lake rejuvenating.

No one noticed when one of their number fell asleep. And

no one noticed when their difficulty at the oars silently brought an end to all conversation. But somewhere about the time when tender palms and burning muscles signaled an alarm about the condition of the sea, everyone woke up to their dilemma.

Any semblance to a pleasant evening trip across the lake was gone. Now they were faced with the sudden onslaught of a Galilean storm. Panic levels rose, and so did the harshness in their voices. As the stiff breeze and mounting waves stung their faces with the blowing spray, would-be leaders barked orders to the others. Grab that sail! Tie off those ropes! Hold the rudder steady! Row harder! Row faster!

Short-fused comments that would have stung under normal conditions went unnoticed. Everyone knew what was at stake. With water pouring steadily over the gunwales of the boat and the fury of the storm increasing, hope of making it safely to shore dwindled by the minute.

And there was Jesus sound asleep. Considering all the chaos within the boat and the pounding of the storm-swept sea against the boat, how could He sleep? How could anyone sleep in such perilous conditions?

Why is it that some people can encounter the greatest of life's trials and remain at rest right through the middle of them? Most of us scamper and scurry and scream and who knows what else trying to bring things under control, trying to get the upper hand.

In the boat that night there was no upper hand to be had! There was no controlling the rage of the sea. Each man on board knew stories of people who had been trapped by unexpected storms on the Sea of Galilee never to return. Their panic was legitimate. And there was Jesus sleeping, doing nothing to help, leaving His disciples to fight these life-threatening battles on their own. What kind of Savior could sleep when His followers needed him so badly?

It's easy to imagine some of those passengers growing a little miffed at Jesus that night. Why would He allow them— no, why would He *send* them across the lake on this evening? Wouldn't He have known what was coming? At the very least, couldn't He have warned them of what was ahead or promised them a safe outcome? Why wasn't He doing anything to help now?

Questions like these fill our private conversations when life is torn apart by uncontrollable storms. They stew within until, just like what transpired next in that waterlogged boat, all the pent-up emotion of our worst fears explodes. "Teacher, don't You care that we are about to drown!" "How can You sleep when we need You so badly?" "How can You abandon us to face these waves alone?" "Are You going to do something before it is too late?" "Jesus, don't You care?" (Look closely at Mark 4:35-41 and you'll see that this is exactly the sentiment with which the disciples awoke Jesus that evening.)

Have you ever wondered why they waited so long to awake Jesus? The more I think about all they were facing and about Jesus' physical presence there with them, the more I am floored by their actions. Why did they battle that unmanageable storm so long in their own strength? How could they stumble and step over Jesus and ignore Him when they had no hope apart from Him? Furthermore, why is it so easy for us to see the flaws in the disciples' panic-driven efforts and miss those flaws in ourselves when we make the same error?

When they could stand it no longer, they awoke Jesus. The Scriptures tell us that Jesus got up immediately and rebuked the wind and the waves; and at the sound of His voice the deadly storm abated. The torment was instantly transformed into a sea of tranquillity. One moment the disciples were battered and drenched by a lethal storm, and the next moment they were at rest in the midst of absolute peace. Jesus was the key to peace, and He had been right there with them in the boat all along.

Their experience is filled with radical implications for the deity of Christ. However, it also illustrates the path to peace for each of us. Quite simply, the key to peace is always found in the active work of Christ. It is always available from the Savior who is there in the boat with us. Regardless of how things look, He is present and eager to work.

PROMISES OF PEACE

The great thing about stories like this one is that they remind us of the power of Christ. For the disciples, this was one of the moments that convinced them of His deity. For us, this miracle on the lake gives weight to the promises of peace that we cherish. However, at the same time, the problem with stories like this is that the storms we face are rarely resolved in the same way.

It's easy to read what happened to the disciples and rejoice for them. It's also easy to recognize theological implications about the identity of Christ inherent in this episode. But when we are the ones in the middle of a raging sea, when our boat is the one taking on too much water, when the wind and waves are overwhelming us, when God is quiet and circumstances are beyond our control, peace is hard to find.

All we can do is cling to His promises.

> *"Come to me, all you who are weary and burdened, and I will give you rest. Take my yoke upon you and learn from me, for I am gentle and humble in heart, and you will find rest for your souls. For my yoke is easy and my burden is light."*

(Matthew 11:28-30)

"I have told you these things, so that in me you may have peace. In this world you will have trouble. But take heart! I have overcome the world."

(John 16:33)

And the peace of God, which transcends all understanding, will guard your hearts and your minds in Christ Jesus.

(Philippians 4:7)

There is a sweetness about these promises that draws us to them repeatedly. They touch us at our point of deep need, and they promise God's active involvement within us. When life is out of control, we may want God to change our circumstances, to make the difficult things go away. But the truth is, we need Him to work within us. When life is tough, which it often is, we need to have God create a calm center within us, just as he did for the disciples on the Sea of Galilee.

However, just reading, memorizing, or reciting these promises like some biblical mantra doesn't make peace happen. They are not some kind of spiritual fairy dust to be liberally sprinkled over anyone in need. They point out what is available. They remind us that God is still in the boat and still able to bring peace in spite of a raging storm. They remind us to come to the source. And interestingly, these great promises actually increase our desire to experience this peace that surpasses understanding.

So we have to ask, what is the process for acquiring this peace that we long for so badly? Is it simple to find, or is that a complex and arduous task? God has shown us how to obtain His peace. The process is seen in Philippians 4, in the verse immediately preceding the promise of "the peace of God, which transcends all understanding."

*Do not be anxious about anything, but in everything, by
prayer and petition, with thanksgiving, present your
requests to God.*

(Philippians 4:6)

A DIVINE TRANSACTION

I wouldn't be surprised to find you thinking, "Pray? That's it?
Tried it before! Hundreds of times—and it's not enough!" I
understand how you may be tempted to react that way, but
hang on; suspend any doubts you may have for a moment.
Unfortunately, when a passage or promise becomes very
familiar we often mistake what is simple for something simplistic. The heart of Philippians 4:6 is anything but a naive or
simplistic solution.

Prayer comes naturally when we are in trouble. Yet, anxi-
ety-focused prayers are rarely the kind that produce peace.
More typically they are prayers that fixate on the problem and
define in detail every possible "woe is me" scenario.
(Remember Jehoshaphat and how differently he prayed?) The
Apostle Paul, here in Philippians 4, is describing a very different process. He is outlining a divine transaction that occurs
through the vehicle of prayer.

He says we are to take whatever makes us stressed, whatever
causes us to be anxious, and present it to God. To take what we
are facing and hand it over to Him through prayer. To say, "Lord,
here it is. I cannot do anything about it, and I can't stand it any
longer." Through the process of prayer we are to relinquish our
hold on the circumstances beyond our control, those areas
where we have little if any power, and give them to the One who
has unlimited power.

Then God gives us His promised response, His part of the

transaction. As we hand things over to Him, He offers us His peace in exchange. This divine transaction is a double win for us. God offers to exchange His peace for the things that make us stressed. He is offering to take responsibility for those circumstances beyond our control and in their place to establish His unbelievable peace in our hearts and lives.

This is an unbeatable bargain. If we give God ownership of the people, circumstances, fears, decisions, etc. that are causing us to churn with anxious thoughts—the things that rob us of peace—He will give us the gift of His perfect peace. This peace of His is better, deeper, richer, and more substantial than anything we can imagine or describe. To receive such a gift in exchange for the garbage we are handing Him sounds too good to be true, but it's not! It is true—and available to everyone who will ask.

What's more, there is no limit to His offer! God has told us that *anytime anything* causes us to become anxious, He would like us to hand it off to Him. In *everything* we are to come to Him with prayers and petitions. To paraphrase His offer, "If anything is important to you, it is important to Me. Hand it over to Me in exchange for My peace."

THE KEY IS OWNERSHIP

Have you ever bought or sold a car? After haggling and dickering over details of the purchase, payments are made and paperwork is signed. One crucial piece of that paperwork is the title to the car. As a seller it is the last thing you hand to the buyer, because once signed away the car is no longer yours. As a buyer, it is the consummation of the deal and the moment at which this new vehicle begins to belong to you.

Once the sale is over, who is responsible for the car? The new owner, of course. What if the new owner decides to let the car deteriorate by not performing routine maintenance—whose problem is that? Obviously his. What if someone purchases a car from you and six months later plows into the rear end of another car? No one could come after you claiming you were responsible, could they? Of course not. But why?

The simple principle is that whoever owns the car is responsible for the car. It is his or her car to care for, maintain, and drive responsibly. If the new owner chooses to be negligent, the previous owner is not at all responsible, because it is no longer his car and therefore no longer his problem.

So what's the point? When we exercise the kind of prayer described in Philippians 4:6, we are signing away the title or deed of our concerns and are giving them to the Lord for His care. God has not only offered to take ownership of these matters, He has offered to "pay us" for the privilege: to give us His peace. Once signed away, our former concerns now belong to Him, not to us.

Now then, who is responsible for the outcome of things— the former or the new owner? Who needs to exercise concern over them—the old or the new owner? Whose resources will be used to meet the demands ahead—the previous or the current owner?

Why do we continue to worry over things that no longer belong to us?

Could it be that even though we have transferred the title, we are operating as if it is still our responsibility to single-handedly take care of whatever we face? But once we have transferred the title, that which it represents no longer belongs to us. Spiritually speaking, we must let the new owner be responsible for what is now rightfully His. When things are no longer our responsibility and we are no longer dependent on our own limited wisdom or resources, we are free from anxiety. Not only is there then the relief that accompanies freedom from the responsibilities associated with ownership, but there is a newly acquired peace replacing the former stress.

When the disciples could no longer cope with the fear and strain of their circumstances on the lake, they awoke Jesus. He not only heard their cries but met their need. When they confessed their need and turned to the Savior, they discovered the peace that had been available all along.

RECURRING TURMOIL HAS UNIQUE VALUE

At this point you may be thinking, "Wait . . . I've tried that before. I prayed about something that was distressing me and felt better for a little while. But then, next thing I knew, the peace was gone, and I was all churned up inside again."

If we are going to honestly apply the lessons of peace in Philippians 4, we must wrestle with the recurring turmoil that accompanies any significant issue or trial. Acquiring peace is not a one-time act.

There is no magic formula to be prayed that instantly resolves all dimensions of our anxiety once and for all. People who find that a prolonged dilemma creates a recurring struggle to find peace have been made to feel guilty about their supposed lack of faith. Yet, the battle to discover peace and maintain a calm center is for most (if not all) of us a daily one. In fact, this promise of peace even addresses the recurring battle! Look again closely at God's gracious promise.

> *Do not be anxious about anything, but in everything,*
> *by prayer and petition, with thanksgiving, present your*
> *requests to God. And the peace of God, which transcends*
> *all understanding, will guard your hearts and your minds*
> *in Christ Jesus.*

Did you see it? There is no indication that this kind of prayer is a one-time thing. In the first place, Paul tells us that anytime any concern creates any anxiety for any reason we are invited to bring that concern to the throne and give it to the Lord. There is no limit! There are no restrictions! There is no hint of shame if your concern is the same today as it was yesterday, the day before, the week before, or a decade before. "Do not be anxious about anything, but in everything . . ." Therefore, should you ever find yourself questioning the appropriateness of your prayers, tell yourself the truth from God's perspective and refuse to listen to anyone who leads you to believe differently.

If that weren't enough to give you freedom in the daily battle, there is another, even more significant insight for the battle to find peace at the end of verse 7. Paul writes that the "peace of God . . . will guard your hearts and minds."

What he literally says is that God's incredible peace will stand as a sentry over your heart and mind, performing the duties of any good guard: protection and warning. Protection is easy to understand. God's peace will protect us from the whirlwind of stresses surrounding us. But what about the element of warning?

When we begin to lose our sense of peace, it is as if the sentry is sounding the alarm, alerting us to the need for beefing up our battle-readiness—warning us that while there is time we should return to the source for reinforcement. In short, when peace falters, our sentry is driving us back to our knees, to the place of power and strength, for the battle at hand is too great to be fought alone.

Some enemies at the gate will be dealt with directly by this on-duty-officer—"peace." Other confrontations are too big; and so, like any wise sentry, the guardian of our heart sounds an alarm that is intended to drive us back into the throne room to the foot of the cross, where we can find rest and refuge for our souls.

The result? Ongoing turmoil has the ability to draw us into

a greater experience of intimacy and dependency on our Lord than anything else. Far from being a sign of spiritual weakness and a reason for guilt, the recurring absence of peace is a warning alarm meant to keep us from doing battle in our own strength. In short, times of turmoil are much more likely to produce intimacy with God than are times of triumph. God's unsurpassed peace that actively stands guard over our hearts and minds is a key to making this happen.

Each of us faces times when circumstances are beyond our control and God is too quiet for comfort. The daily grind of those circumstances wears us down and stresses us out. Emotionally, this is a midnight ride on a stormy sea with no way out and no relief in sight. In those moments, in the depth of your cry for peace, you must recognize that the One who has all authority, all power, and infinite compassion is in the boat with you. He never asks you to cross the sea alone. In fact, He offers to give you His peace if only you will give Him your concerns.

Why not take a moment right now and hand things over to Him anew? Make the exchange. Allow His peace to become the guardian of your heart. There are no substitutes, and there is no wiser place to turn.

THE BOTTOM LINE

Peace comes when we relinquish ownership
of what we face to the One who has unlimited ability,
inexhaustible resources, and impeccable timing.

PART TWO

ENEMIES OF REST

*Because we
need to be prepared for the
battles we'll face*

CHAPTER SIX

When the Sirens Sing

Every muscle in his tan, lean body strained and tore against the ropes that bound him to the mast. Cruel, coarse hemp cut easily into his flesh, the painful wounds made worse by the sting of salty spray. Drenched with sweat, a literal picture of human agony, Ulysses cried out in desperation to be cut loose. His cries went ignored.

His mental anguish grew so severe, his crew feared their captain would never survive this self-imposed ordeal. No caring person would let it continue! It was inhuman to allow this torture. Yet, all they could do was turn their heads and avoid eye contact. After all, by his own orders Ulysses stood lashed against the mast of his ship in order to sample the alluring beauty of the Sirens' music.

In this manner the great Ulysses heard the song of the Sirens and survived their hypnotic call. The beauty, the allure, the seductive power of the Sirens had drawn man after man to his death. Every sailor knew the tales. Every sailor was well aware of the danger of these seas. Only fools sailed unprepared through these waters. Only idiots shunned the warnings, believing they were strong enough to resist the temptation of the Sirens' call. Without exception, the beautiful, hypnotic strains of the Sirens' music led to brutal destruction by violent waves against razor-like rocks on shore.

Ulysses was no fool. Neither he nor his crew had immunity to the Sirens' spell. They were no less vulnerable than others who had sacrificed their lives in these waters. Therefore, he ordered his men to plug their ears, effectively blocking out the music. However, with a flair worthy of any superhero, he devised a way in which he himself might listen and survive. He commanded his men to strap him to the mast with the strongest of ropes and then sail on through these dangerous seas. No matter what he said or what he did, they were to disregard his pleas.

This classic tale from Greek mythology offers a lesson for us. During those days when we sail through turbulent waters, when circumstances rob us of our ability to rest, we will hear the Sirens sing. The music we hear will have voices just as seductive and just as deadly as those Ulysses heard. Our Sirens are usually the internal voices of impatience crying out to us with words of fear, panic, doubt, embarrassment, frustration, or even anger. The more difficult our circumstances, or the more desperate the issues before us, the louder they cry.

So the question is, when we hear the Sirens sing, what will hold us back? What will keep us from falling prey to the deceitful beauty of their music?

In every case their cries tempt us to compromise our convictions. They fog our thinking and occupy us with delusions of self-sufficiency. They lure us into rationalizing away our priorities. They generate powerful doubts about God's character and ability. They attempt to short-circuit our faith.

You recognize their message; you've heard it many times. "Rein in this unrealistic, childish talk of faith and do something practical." "Do anything, but don't just sit there." "Take that job offer even though the hours, location, or travel don't match the needs of your family. How can you wait any longer for something better?" "Haven't you been single long enough? Accept that marriage proposal—or make one—even if he or she isn't quite right for you." "Stretch the truth in that sales pitch. Integrity won't put food on the table." "Move on to a different ministry. You can't waste your time waiting for a better opportunity any longer." What is the message in the song of impatience you're hearing these days?

When you hear the Sirens sing, stop and listen closely. You'll also hear the echo of waves pounding against the rocks. Count on it—there is *always* a painful price to be paid for impatience. In the midst of the pain and panic of the moment, the lure of impatient solutions appears to make sense. However, the aftermath of those alternatives *never* matches the promise of their appeal and typically leads to even greater distress.

WHEN YOU HEAR THEIR SONG, WHAT WILL YOU DO?

The story of Ulysses creatively illustrates the intense dynamics we feel when circumstances throw our lives off-balance. Yet, we need examples that are real, not myth. We need to see principles and patterns lived out by real people. We need to see examples of people with flesh and bones. People that bruise and break but who made it through situations like our own. When we find ourselves struggling with turbulent emotions caused by delay and uncertainty, we yearn for the encouragement that comes from the testimony of fellow strugglers.

That is one of the things I love about the Scriptures. God was working in the lives of real people as they trudged through the real stuff of life. And He preserved their stories for our benefit. Their lives sometimes got messy, and He shows us their muddied laundry. They also experienced personal victory, and God tells us the good news of their triumph without overstated glamorization. He never sugarcoated or doctored up the record of their lives. Rather, He laid it all out for our examination and our encouragement. He knows we learn from people who not only teach by precept but by example. He knows we learn both from successes and from failures.

Therefore, let's consider two men whose lives have been immortalized in Scripture. Two men who heard the Sirens' call to abandon the wait. Two men who—to their own detriment—took matters into their own hands in the wrong way at the wrong time. Two men just like us who heard the Sirens' song of impatience and gave in to its lies. Two men who demonstrate the way deceptive compromises drive us away from greater rest and lead to increased agony. Two men who are just a sample of all who share similar stories. Though these are negative examples, the influence of their testimonies is anything but negative. Their testimonies help us see ourselves in a fresh light and provide ammunition for our own battle with impatience.

It has been said that few things motivate us like the fear of adverse consequences. The imminent possibility of pain is a great motivator to keep us from giving up. No one likes pain. To that end, the cumulative power of these case histories might give you just the boost you need when your resistance to the Sirens' voices wanes.

JACOB: AN HEIR WITH NO INHERITANCE

Meet Jacob. Grandson to the great Abraham. Son of the miracle-child Isaac. Heir of the promises. And twin brother to that favorite son, Esau—the one standing directly in his way. You would think that anyone with a grandfather like Abraham and a grandmother like Sarah would know enough of the power of God to have a dynamite faith. How could the oft-repeated stories learned around evening campfires not fill his spirit with unshakable confidence in God's ability? However, Jacob heard the Sirens sing and discovered the pain of those who succumb to their deceit.

His story really began before his birth. Twins are always noteworthy, but the birth of Jacob and Esau was unique. During the uncomfortable days of her pregnancy, Rebekah experienced one of those history-making encounters with the living God. God told her that contrary to custom the older twin would serve the younger. The younger would be the son of promise. The younger would inherit the blessing, the place of priority in the family line, and the majority of the estate. The younger, not the elder, would continue the messianic line. Jacob, the younger son, would become the firstborn son in God's economy.

Now, put yourself in Jacob's shoes for a few moments. Your favorite boyhood story was the one about your mother's personal encounter with God. Asking her to repeat every detail of the story and the promises accompanying it became a bedtime ritual. Yet now, as an adult, you are tired of clinging to a familiar promise faced with an impossible obstacle.

That obstacle was Esau.

Esau was the firstborn. He was Dad's favorite and was becoming more so every year. You became a confidant to your mother, but that did little to secure the benefits of the promise. Your father's heart was bent toward Esau. Unless something happened soon, Esau would receive the blessing, the inheritance, and the family position. You've relied on a divine promise, but God's miraculous promises appear to be jeopardized by your father, who seems ill-inclined to cooperate.

Maintaining faith is easy when you can see how God is at work. Faith makes sense as long as you can spot a few possible ways for God to pull things out. Confidence in God's Word and God's ways can be defended when circumstances are not completely bleak. But when a situation looks absolutely hopeless, when you feel completely helpless, when every avenue for change is beyond your control, even mustard-seed faith looks foolish. Illogical. Silly.

Months and years passed, and the Sirens began to sing. Their song of impatience carried that familiar tune of rationalization. Time and distance between Jacob and us make it easy to be skeptical of their lyrics, but for Jacob and for all who battle with hopeless circumstances, their words have a haunting appeal.

"Jacob, there must be a way. You're smarter than Esau. After all, God's reputation is at stake in this, too! Maybe you should be bold and bring God's promise to life yourself. God made you clever, didn't He? Use that gift of cleverness to make things happen. Does God expect you to wait for a miracle when you could take care of things yourself? God promised it, you deserve it, so just go for it! No matter what it takes."

Jacob listened . . . soon the deed was done . . . the younger twin tricked the older into giving him his birthright . . . and great was the hemorrhage in his family.

It happened in this way: When Isaac was very old and nearly blind, it was time to pass on the blessing—*to Esau*. So he sent Esau hunting for appropriate game, the kind a feast celebrating an occasion like this deserved. Meanwhile, Jacob and Rebekah, in a panic over what was taking place, connived a way to deceive the aging Isaac. Masquerading in goatskins, lying about his identity, and offering a special feast from the flock, Jacob tricked his father into granting him the blessing intended for Esau. *Crash!* The deed was done, and sharp were the rocks.

Lying, cheating, and stealing for a good cause? It sounds like popular advice in today's generation. But because Jacob short-circuited God's plan and God's timing with his own rationalized behavior, the payoff was painful. Consider this:

- Jacob fled to a distant land out of fear of Esau's retaliation. He stayed stuck there for twenty years!
- Those twenty years were years of total separation from his family. He missed the death of both parents and never had the chance to introduce them to his family. His folks never met their grandchildren and vice versa. He missed twenty years of important family events because of his self-inflicted exile.
- When it came time to return to his homeland, he trembled at the thought of meeting his brother again. In fact, he expected that his brother might kill him on sight.
- His own children engaged in similar treachery by selling Joseph, his favorite son, into slavery. He suffered the same pain he had inflicted on his own father—the pain of treachery among his own children.
- Furthermore, the history of the Jews—the story of his family—was peppered by conflict with the descendants of Esau—the Edomites. Centuries later Jacob's descendants were still paying the price for his schemes.

During turbulent times, when circumstances are beyond your control, be on guard for those voices calling you to rationalize your behavior. Often what appears to be a short-cut that you can easily maneuver is a tortuous path toward irreversible pain and heartache. Jacob's story is a story of lifelong turmoil.

And if the relational pain he encountered wasn't enough, his impatience also kept him from experiencing God's miraculous handiwork. Had he not panicked, he would have seen God do the work of fulfilling His promises in His own time and in His own way. Jacob would have witnessed a supernatural solution to a human predicament. He would have been able to pass on valuable lessons of God's timing and faithfulness to every generation. He would have avoided another legacy of family conflict. And on top of it all, none of us will ever know how God would have otherwise intervened (at least not in this life).

SAUL: A KING WITHOUT A KINGDOM

What more could you possibly ask for or ever hope to find in a king? Humble. A natural-born leader. Even tall, dark, and handsome. Saul was the ideal choice in everyone's eyes. Assisted by the godly counsel of Samuel and buoyed by the eagerness of the people to establish themselves as a nation, Saul was bound for greatness. But when the Sirens sang, he lost it all.

Impatience is a formidable adversary. Sometimes in the midst of disconcerting situations our impatience pressures us to compromise our convictions. At other times we hear the temptation to rationalize our behavior. And at still other times the piercing wail of panic becomes our nemesis.

Saul sacrificed his kingdom on the altar of impatience. Simply put, he couldn't stand the wait any longer. He couldn't stand that unbearable sense of being out of control that always accompanies indefinite delay. In the wrong place at the wrong time Saul made a wrong choice. He refused to wait any longer and took matters into his own hands. It was a painful and a costly choice.

Circumstances may be different, but the dynamics feel the same for the unemployed person waiting for a callback on that last job interview. The single man or woman who feels the pressures as they look for Mrs. or Mr. Right. The husband and wife who find themselves stuck in sour economic times while trying to sell a home. It is easy to begin to panic. Being patient during a long delay can be as awful for us as it was for Saul. Our similar experiences make it easy to empathize with him.

Saul was engaged in the conflict of his career against the

Philistines, those oppressive neighbors to the southeast. The ability of his young nation to live independently of foreign influence was at stake. God's promises to establish His kingdom were on the line. The confidence of the people hung in the balance. So Saul listened to the counsel of Samuel.

> *"Go down ahead of me to Gilgal . . . but you must*
> *wait seven days until I come to you and tell you what you*
> *are to do."*
>
> (1 Samuel 10:8)

There was just one problem with this. While Saul and his men were waiting for Samuel, the Philistines were organizing themselves for decisive victory. These Philistines were certainly not going to wait seven more days before attacking God's people!

> *The Philistines assembled to fight Israel, with three*
> *thousand chariots, six thousand charioteers, and soldiers as*
> *numerous as the sand on the seashore.*
>
> (1 Samuel 13:5-6)

To put this in today's terms: "The Philistines used this waiting period to gather 3,000 armored tanks and their best-trained tank crews. They brought in thousands of battle-hungry Marines. And they prepared to finish off Israel's 2,000 foot soldiers."

Contrast the scene in the Philistine camp with that of Saul's forces. While the Philistines were fine-tuning their massive fighting machine, the Israelites were waiting around for Samuel to arrive. Every day that Saul waited, the Philistines sharpened the teeth of their plans. Every day that Saul waited, the Israelites grew more nervous and apprehensive. Every day that Saul waited, the Philistines were plotting a better strategy and were obtaining better reconnaissance. Every day that Saul waited, the Israelites watched their readiness to fight disintegrate into an eagerness to run. Ultimately Saul's men were overrun with fear.

> Saul remained at Gilgal, and all the troops with him
> were quaking with fear. . . . He waited seven days . . .
> but Samuel did not come to Gilgal, and Saul's men
> began to scatter.

(1 Samuel 13:7b-8)

If the Sirens had been singing their song of panic and impatience before, they now turned up the volume to ear-shattering levels. How could Saul afford to wait any longer? Why not take matters into his own hands? After all, the future of the nation was at stake! Samuel had promised to be here on the seventh day, and it *was now* the seventh day. "If he doesn't come now," you can almost hear Saul thinking, "my men will be gone, and the battle will be lost before it begins."

> So he said, "Bring me the burnt offering and the fellowship
> offerings." And Saul offered up the burnt offering [himself].
> Just as he finished making the offering Samuel arrived, and
> Saul went out to greet him.

(1 Samuel 13:9-10)

Notice what took place here. Saul was so overcome by his fear of further delay that he usurped his place before God and offered the sacrifice himself. In fact, Saul was going to offer several sacrifices, the burnt offering and the fellowship offerings; but Samuel arrived before he even started the fellowship offerings. Unwilling to wait just a few more minutes, Saul surrendered everything on the altar of impatience.

After Saul's anemic attempt at excusing what he'd done, Samuel interrupted to confront him with his unwillingness to obey the Lord's command.

> *"You acted foolishly. You have not kept the command the* LORD *your God gave you . . . now your kingdom will not endure."*

(1 Samuel 13:13-14)

The waters churned, the Sirens sang, Saul gave in, and the rocky shore of impatience claimed another victim. The price of his public disobedience and lack of faith was public removal from the place of leadership. Saul continued to rule for a time, but God's hand of blessing moved on to another—to a young musician who sang to an audience of sheep.

Ulysses could place wax in the ears of his men, but the voices that lure us to the rocks are usually internal. No wax can stop their sound. So, what are we to do?

First of all, there is great truth in the saying that to be forewarned is to be forearmed. The point of this chapter has been to heighten your sensitivity to the voices of impatience that will call you away from your moorings. Beware of those voices that will tempt you to short-circuit your confidence in God's ability and timing.

Second, God has designed us to be people who live in relationship with one another. Ulysses instructed his men to lash him to the mast, and we have people who will stand by us. Often the most effective way to diffuse the power of the Sirens' music is to share the battle you face with others. Tell them of the temptation you're facing to compromise your convictions. Ask them to evaluate your thoughts about rationalizing your behavior.

And be honest with them about the pain of your impatience. Their counsel and support might serve as the ropes that hold you to the mast.

Above all, tell yourself the truth. God can be trusted whether you see Him at work or not. His character is intact when you sense His handiwork and when you don't. His timing is always right, and His methods are always a perfect fit. But your impatience will short-circuit His work and most likely cause you to pay a painful price. So, be on guard!

THE BOTTOM LINE

Trusting God because a desirable outcome
seems probable is not really trusting *Him* at all—
it is trusting in probabilities.

CHAPTER SEVEN

The Quagmire of Discontent

As I write this chapter I cannot help but think about a good friend of mine. He is a gifted and godly man stuck in a job situation that hurts him every day. I have tremendous respect for the integrity of his work ethic. He gives himself completely to his job and to the people with whom he works. The essence of the job is one that he likes, but I know the internal turmoil he faces every morning as he arrives at work.

By personality, training, experience, and ability he is an ideal candidate for permanent promotion to an area of greater responsibility. Yet, as a result of internal politics he has been cut out of the loop. Slowly but surely, and not so subtly, responsibilities that were formerly his have been taken away and given to others. His coworkers see this and are frustrated by the reduced influence he is currently allowed. According to their story, the whole environment is more unpleasant and ineffective because of these changes.

The process hurts. Each day as he sees problems arise that he is capable of meeting but is not allowed to address, he is reminded of the way he's been sidelined. Transferring to another location would be a good option, but opportunities are few and far between. So every day is another reminder that his abilities are not used, his opinions not valued, and his hopes for the future tarnished. Quite simply, he is stuck—both now and for the foreseeable future.

At the core of all this is a daily battle to maintain a godly contentment. This not only involves the simple issues of contentment that reflect material wants, but the deep-water stuff. This battle for contentment challenges my friend's entire outlook on life. Maybe you're in a similar spot, the kind over which you have no control and no way out. I've been there. It seems most of us have at one time or another. In times like these we dance on a tightrope. We try to keep our balance, but discontent is like gravity, constantly pulling at us so that the slightest nudge, the slightest surprise, sends us crashing.

Discontent is a voracious enemy that extends its tentacles and threatens to poison every area of one's life.

Anytime your circumstances are less than desirable, you are a candidate for discontent. Anytime you find yourself distressed over what you don't have or can't do, beware. Anytime you are stuck in one of life's waiting room experiences, keep your antennae up. Discontent is crouching nearby to squeeze the life from your joy, your outlook, and your faith.

You'll know you are heading for such a battle when you find the watchwords of discontent flowing through your lips. Consider the following as a sample list of verbal red flags, warning signs to alert you to the enemy lurking in the shadows.

"If only . . ."
"But everyone else is . . ."
"Everyone else has . . ."
"Unless I can . . ."

"Without this . . ."
"Not until . . ."
"It's not fair that . . ."

Common words? Sure. Still, they all share a common theme. We use them when we think something is missing or wrong and that we will not be OK until it is acquired, achieved, arranged for, etc.

Learning to stand strong when God is silent and the circumstances of life scream for attention means dealing with issues of contentment. The secret of contentment is neither mystical nor mysterious, but simple and straightforward. Unfortunately, we have often heard the wrong message and have been sent down the wrong road in search of contentment.

Contentment is a familiar theme, but much of the common advice we hear has the potential of making matters worse. There are at least two familiar roads we travel in the false hope that they will lead to contentment.

THE FALSE ROAD OF CIRCUMSTANTIAL DELIVERANCE

The road of circumstantial deliverance is one that no one really needs to teach us about. It is a road that comes naturally. But it is also a road that sets us up for greater heartache than ever. It could be stated something like this:

The key to contentment lies in my circumstances. Therefore, if my circumstances would just change, everything would be OK.

Real-life variations could sound like this: "If only I made a little more money . . ." "After we move to a new area where the pace of life is different . . ." "As soon as my boss recognizes my real value and . . ." "After the baby is past this stage . . ." Etc., etc., etc. It is easier and less threatening to look outward, to place our hope on circumstances, than to look for inner causes or solutions.

The truth, however, is that contentment is a matter of spirit, not circumstances. Contentment is born deep within our spirit and works its way outward in spite of our circumstances. Contentment is the ability to accept those circumstances that are beyond our ability to change. It is the ability to be at peace internally and to give ourselves wholeheartedly to the demands of life even when our circumstances are different than we believe they ought to be. If contentment were solely dependent on circumstances, we would be helpless and at times without hope, because some circumstances will not change. Or they actually change for the worse. And even if they change for the better, how long will they remain that way?

If our well-being, our ability to be content, depends on the quality of our circumstances, we are doomed to living lives of endless upheaval. We are doomed to living at the whim and turn of everyone and everything around us. If contentment is dependent on circumstances, then it is not really contentment, but mere comfort. And as soon as our comfort is disturbed, we will be back in the throes of discontent without hope. No, thank you. God must have something better in mind than that.

On a spiritual level, there is an even deeper problem with the circumstantial approach to contentment. It is very possible that we crave for circumstantial comfort so we can step back from the edge of absolute dependency on God. Circumstantial or material well-being has a way of masking our desperate need for God and His work. After all, when life is OK, we feel OK; and if we feel OK, we must surely be OK. Then God is free to devote His time and energy on someone who is needy. When life is going along smoothly, it is easy for us to mistake our well-being for a sign that our spiritual life is healthy as well.

Could it be that circumstantial discontent is a God-given reminder that we are incomplete apart from an active, ongoing relationship with our Creator? Could discontent be one of God's tools to help us discover His ability to meet us at our point of need? Could it be one more method to draw us to the power and presence of His staff when we walk through the valley?

THE FALSE ROAD OF SPIRITUAL FORTITUDE

As contentment is in essence a spiritual matter, people have rightly gone to the Scriptures for answers. Nowhere is this issue more clearly addressed than by the Apostle Paul in Philippians 4:12.

> *I know what it is to be in need, and I know what it is to have plenty. I have learned the secret of being content in any and every situation, whether well fed or hungry, whether living in plenty or in want.*

On one hand, this is a verse that should offer great hope. But on the other hand, I cringe at the way I have heard it taught. Allow me to paraphrase the typical emphasis I have heard from this passage.

I, Paul, have been through every possible circumstance you can imagine. I have had times of plenty and times where the pain of hunger tore me apart. I have stayed in five-star resorts and have been lost at sea for days on end. I have known what it is like to live in genuine comfort and to live in real poverty. I have been thrown out of town with no place to go, and I have been treated like royalty. But through it all I have learned the secret of being content no matter what my circumstances. If I can be content with all I have to face, you should learn to be content, too!

Sound familiar? Sure, it does. The general message we hear about contentment and about this passage is that contentment is basically a matter of willpower. Therefore, go out there and learn to be content. If you struggle with discontent, just stop and be different. If life gives you lemons, make lemonade!

I have heard this emphasis from numerous speakers, writers, and teachers. In fact, just a few weeks before working on this chapter I saw it again in an article written by a well-respected author in a well-respected magazine. The emphasis in its most basic form is simply to learn to be content by forcing yourself to be content. Reach way down deep for some sort of spiritual fortitude and just do it! Trust that God has a plan for your circumstances. Smile—it could be worse! Put on a happy face. After all, millions of people have it a lot worse than you do; so buck up and take it like a man.

Such superspiritualized gobbledygook does not help. In fact, it only makes us feel like spiritual failures because our faith is not strong enough to generate the spiritualized intestinal fortitude that makes us able to withstand the pains and frustrations of living in a fallen world. (Don't even get me started on the misapplied one-a-day version of Romans 8:28.)

The quagmire of discontent is a vile and insidious villain. By claiming that the secret is to make ourselves content—to just do it, we may be appealing to our pride through the back door. Our pride wants us to believe that we can make it on our own. That we are adequate to live and reign at the center of our universe. That given enough time we can work things out on our own. But when it comes to the deeply personal issues of dissatisfaction, most of our struggle ends up being devoted to maintaining appearances—trying to mask the black hole of discontent that is sucking the quality of our relationships, our work, our outlook on life, and our love for God right down the drain.

And when our best second-efforts still fall short, we add the burden of spiritual failure to the struggle with discontent and eventually give up. Who cares whether Paul learned the secret or not. We haven't found it, and everything we've tried hasn't worked. The road to contentment through some form of super-spiritual fortitude leads us off the cliff of despair.

Paul did not say that the secret of contentment was trying harder. There has to be a better way.

A SECRET THAT WORKS

Back to Philippians 4:12. Perhaps it's our identification with the circumstances Paul faced, perhaps it's our fixation on studying Scripture one verse at a time, perhaps it's our own ego-driven desire to conquer all of life's ills on our own instead of being honestly needy—whatever, the secret to contentment has been right there under our noses all along. As a matter of fact, a vast majority have memorized the secret without even knowing it.

Philippians 4:12 includes a hint at some of the situations Paul had to learn to cope with. Reading about them sparks immediate reactions within us as we recall similar tensions and circumstances in our own lives. However, it is easy to be side-tracked by the details of verse 12 and miss the connection with the sentence that immediately follows it. Let me remove a few parenthetical phrases from Paul's original words in verse 12 and add verse 13. You will see the secret of contentment for your-self as it jumps right off the page.

> . . . *I have learned the secret of being content in any and every situation. . . . I can do everything through him who gives me strength.*

Paul did not leave us to sweat over some mysterious secret. He made it plain from the beginning. The secret to contentment is found in the daily, enabling strength of Christ. Through the strength of Christ I can make it through today and whatever it holds. I may be overwhelmed with disappointment, frustrated over the absence of progress, hungry for opportunities that I cannot create out of my own resources, or worn down by any number of contentment-robbing circumstances. But in the midst of my need Christ, who promises me His presence and power, is able to give me enough strength to face the things I have to face today—if I will let him.

Because we are familiar with Philippians 4:13, Paul's point may seem so obvious that we easily miss it. It is not just that we need the strength of Christ to face the major demands of life, though we certainly do. The key to contentment is the daily, enabling power of Christ. There is no magic formula, no quick self-help program, and no gimmick. Relying on the strength of Christ is our only hope for finding the contentment we need to face the demanding and disappointing circumstances of life.

Contentment is not the product of some internal force of will. It comes when we acknowledge our own inadequacy, when we confess our desperation, and when we allow Christ to be enough. Contentment is possible in any and every situation if we will face every day through the strength and presence of Jesus Christ.

This is a learned process.

When Paul said he had "learned the secret of being content," he used an interesting word. He chose a word often used to speak of the difficult learning process people went through when they were initiated into some of the pagan cults of his day. In this context, his word choice hints at the fact that even though the secret is simple, the process of learning to be content is a slow, expanding discovery of what it means to live through the strength of Christ. Learning to live victoriously in any and every type of circumstance is no easy task.

It's funny, really. The empowering presence of Christ is

with all of us who have given our lives to His saving grace. His strength is available in every situation every day. He never leaves us or forsakes us. Yet, when life knocks us over the edge of the cliff and we hang suspended, barely holding on to the end of our rope, we often continue to hang on in our own strength and ability. We may call on the Lord to assist us with the challenge we face, but we still fight to hang on by our own power. When the rope breaks, when our endurance drains beyond the point of exhaustion, when we give up any hope of working things out on our own, when we have no other options remaining, we finally allow ourselves to fall into His hands. We have no other choice. And at the end of our fall, when all other efforts have failed and we collapse into His hands as a final resort, we discover He can provide the strength we needed all along.

When the rope breaks, we are tempted to feel that we have been discarded. That we have been cut loose by God Himself. That somehow we didn't have what it took to carry our share of the weight. Now we must come as needy vessels into the presence of Christ, apologizing for our failure to meet a standard that only our twisted pride believed we were supposed to meet. The truth is, we were desperate and needy from the beginning—it just took a crisis to teach us that was true. God may allow us to fully exhaust our own endurance so that we will rediscover the daily, enabling power of Christ.

The secret of contentment is not found in the product of some heroic self-effort, but in the empowering hands of Christ. Not only is He enough, but He and His power are the only true means at our disposal for obtaining contentment sufficient for any circumstances.

When the rope breaks and our free fall strips away every nuance of pride, we cry out to be caught by the strong hands of our God. Our prayers are neither polished nor polite, but they are real. We confess our absolute desperation. We just need to be caught. And we need to be carried by His strength, because ours is gone.

My experience, the experience of those I know, and, I believe, the testimony of Scripture all agree that when the rope breaks, we discover the presence and power of Christ in a new way. When our resources are depleted, we find ourselves in a position to discover His resources, maybe for the first time.

If we will turn to Christ and confess our need, we will discover victory, not disaster, at the end of our free fall. That victory is the internal renewal stated best in Paul's words, the newfound ability to "do everything through him who gives me strength."

Stop and think about this. Christ's power and presence are there from the first moment we give our lives to Him, not just when all other approaches have failed! So, why do we continually seek to manufacture the strength to be content apart from Him? The secret of contentment is not a matter of internal willpower or superspiritualized fortitude, but of leaning on Christ in "any and every situation, whether well fed or hungry, whether living in plenty or in want."

THE LITTLE GAME WE PLAY

There is a game we play with God at times. When in the midst of unbearable circumstances, we begin to pursue contentment with the belief that once we learn to accept our circumstances, then God will be free to remove them from us. We say things to ourselves like, "If I just learn to accept my singleness, God will send me a husband (or a wife.)" "If I can learn to accept this job that I hate and give it my best, God will be free to provide me with a better one." "If I can just learn the lesson God is trying to teach me in this situation, He will be able to move me on." And on and on it goes.

Bargaining like this is not contentment. It is an attempt to manipulate God through an appearance of contentment. It may be politely masked, but strip away the façade and we are talking about twisting God's arm. We are merely using our battle to achieve contentment as a last resort in our attempt to obtain the unmet wants and needs at the core of our discontent. We are still pursuing circumstantial change under the guise of contentment. And lasting contentment can never be circumstantially based.

Let's be honest. There are times when circumstances do not change. When no husband or wife is coming. When there is no new job. When children do not return to the Lord. When finances remain tight. If our contentment is dependent on changing circumstances in any way, we are looking in the wrong place and are misunderstanding what God has in mind for us.

THE DAILY GRIND

When your circumstances scream for attention and God remains silent, you will battle with discontent. There is no way around it. And this battle will be a daily one. The fresh wind of God's Spirit that carried you through yesterday and the glimmer of possibilities you saw last week will not suffice for the demands of today, let alone tomorrow. The struggle to find contentment and to gain freedom from the poison of discontent is a daily struggle. But the mercies of God are "new every morning" (Lamentations 3:22-23).

Understanding this daily aspect of the battle is essential. For some reason many of us expect to overcome struggles like this in a single step. (As in, "leap tall buildings in a single bound.") Dealing with the quagmire of discontent will be a daily or even hourly battle as you return to the position of need at the feet of your Savior. However, you will find that in that position of need, broken and desperate at His feet, you are in the place of strength, not weakness. *His* strength, not yours.

The strength of Christ is available to you every moment of every day in every type of circumstance. Why carry on in your own strength one moment longer? Allow the daily grind of life to be God's daily tutor, helping you discover greater depths of intimacy, involvement, and insight in your relationship with Him.

It's time we started telling ourselves the truth. We are aliens and sojourners in this life. To believe differently is to believe a lie. God has built us for eternity, and until then the circumstances of this life will never be enough to fully satisfy us. Our search for contentment is a constant reminder of where our real hope lies, where our real home is, and where our real strength comes from in the meantime.

THE BOTTOM LINE

Contentment is not the product of heroic self-effort, but is found only in the daily, enabling power of Christ.

CHAPTER EIGHT

The Roller Coaster of Discouragement

Every father thrives on opportunities to share the adventures of life with his son. These are rites of passage. Moments of pride. Times to be cherished. And so it was as my son and I approached one of those simple thrills of life, the roller coaster. There we were, standing in line, his eyes full of trust, mine filled with anticipation. Up ahead lay two and a half minutes of high-speed twisting, turning, climbing, dropping, stomach-launching bumps and dips. Within sight was the initial four-story climb and its familiar clickety-clack, clickety-clack, chug-strain-chug. I knew that just over that crest was a high-speed cascade down a nearly vertical slope designed by someone with a very callused conscience. What fun we were to have! We were men on a mission.

My son and I were alone together because my daughter was too young and my wife hates these things. He, on the other hand, had loved the other coasters in the park. So it seemed logical, now that he just squeaked by the minimum height requirement, that he and I would soar together up and over and around the wooden tracks of this adrenaline machine. Only one problem. He was too young and I didn't recognize it.

From the initial lurch down the backside of the infamous first hill, I knew I had made a mistake. Those two and a half minutes were the longest of my life. He sat there hardly breathing, making no sound, staring straight ahead with eyes that seemed to suggest he was praying for the immediate return of Christ. If the wind weren't drying my eyes faster than human tear ducts can keep up, I might have cried.

What I thought would be fun, he found to be terrifying. While I knew that these rides are generally safe, he feared being ejected at any moment. Though any other lap around this star attraction would have been a source of joy for me, this trip was pure agony. When we finally pulled into the station to disembark and stepped again onto *terra firma*, I felt as if I had just survived a firsthand taste of eternity in that place of perpetual heat. Ryan just held my hand and said nothing until we found the source of every child's security—Mom.

Discouragement is often like that roller coaster ride was for my son. We climb a hill, work long and hard on a project, seek to conquer new goals, invest our energies in a worthy effort— and then when we least expect it, the plunge downhill catches us off-guard and sends us to the edge of our seats for a ride we cannot control. The twists and turns hold so much centrifugal force, they threaten to throw us overboard. The speed of the downhill plunge causes us to believe there can be no option but a colossal crash when we reach the bottom. When there is a moment to catch our breath, the quietness makes us worry about what unseen terrors lie ahead. And when the ride is at its very worst, it seems there is a very real possibility it will never end.

The third of our internal enemies, discouragement, has the ability to catch us by surprise and throw our outlook on life into a tailspin. Like the pain of impatience and the quagmire of discontent, discouragement works from the inside out, distorting our perspective and destabilizing our confidence in the character of God.

Discouragement has the ability to short-circuit our faith, warp our vision, fog our thinking, and cripple our understanding of God's promises. Working behind the scenes while our primary energies are spent elsewhere, discouragement has done great damage by the time its presence is felt. Discouragement drains our hope, enthusiasm, sense of purpose, and more—those qualities that keep us motivated for the challenges of daily life. It takes us on a ride for which we are rarely prepared.

Seasons of discouragement are invariably times when God seems silent. Were He to intervene and unveil the details of His perspective or purpose, the struggles would be bearable. In times of silence they are severe.

Therefore, during times like this we need to ask ourselves, how can we lean toward God rather than pull away from Him? What can we do to keep our balance during the ups and downs of discouraging times? What will help us draw upon the credibility of our faith instead of questioning its validity? Where in the Scriptures can we find help when our emotions betray us? How can we demonstrate a substantial faith to the world around us when the circumstances of life are tearing us apart?

MEET A FELLOW STRUGGLER

Allow me to introduce a fellow passenger on the roller coaster of discouragement. He knew what it was to pour his life into serving others only to receive a crushing blow of discouragement as the reward for his labors. Yet, in his struggles he demonstrated the key to vital faith during times of deep disappointment. His name is Jeremiah. To fully appreciate his insights, you must understand a bit of his story.

Jeremiah the prophet was responsible for two of our Old Testament gold mines. The book that bears his name walks us through forty years of ministry. He was commissioned to warn Israel of God's impending judgment in the hope that there would be a change of heart. There wasn't. Lamentations, his second book, is a revealing glimpse into the heart of a man whose message and ministry went ignored by God's people. It also outlines the source of his stability during the most difficult of discouragements.

From the very beginning Jeremiah knew both the exhilaration of divine calling and the humiliation of rejection. He knew the promise of God and the ridicule of God's people. When God called him to be His prophet in Israel, that call was given in person. No intermediaries. No human passing of a mantle. Direct divine intervention was the bottom line on Jeremiah's resumé. But even then the only guarantee accompanying this supernatural calling was a promise of hardship and rejection.

Jeremiah was told from the outset that the people of Israel, his congregation if you will, would not listen to him. They would reject him. Worse, "They will *fight against you*" (Jeremiah 1:19, italics mine)

Did you catch that? Jeremiah was called by God to a ministry that would show little success. He would spend his life faithfully obeying his calling, and yet there would be little or nothing to show for it. The coming judgment would not be averted, the spiritual decline of the nation would not be reversed, Jeremiah's authority as a prophet would receive little or no respect, and his own quality of life would be anything but comfortable. He would never send holiday cards detailing the growth of his ministry. He would never have anything to brag about when attending conferences for local prophets. He was called to a difficult position among an obstinate people.

To be even more specific and to catch a fuller sense of what life was like for Jeremiah, consider the following summary of his disappointments. And while you are at it, try to imagine yourself in his shoes. Try to imagine that this is the response you were receiving to your life's work!

- More than once he was beaten because they hated his message and its implications (20:2; 37:15).
- After one of his beatings he was put in the stocks near a popular temple entrance. In the very spot where the God he served was to be worshiped, he was subjected to public humiliation (20:2-3).
- After another beating he was thrown into a prison dungeon, "where he remained a long time." And lest we think this dungeon was a quaint little downstairs room for VIP guests, guess again. Jeremiah later pled with King Zedekiah not to be returned to the dungeon because it would certainly lead to his death. This was brutal treatment (37:15-20).
- He was arrested on a number of occasions because his words were politically offensive to leaders who had lost their spiritual bearings (37:13; 38:6).
- He was mocked. And the very words people used to mock him were words God had given him to say (20:10). (The name God told him to give Passhur, the chief official of the temple, was "Magor-Missabib," which means "terror on every side." This was the very phrase that became a public taunt for Jeremiah. See Jeremiah 20:3-4 and 20:10.)
- In opposition to Jeremiah, a whole band of false prophets arose that prophesied peace and good news. These "good news boys" received tremendous respect and influence, while Jeremiah received only pressure to follow their lead. While he labored for the truth, they were rewarded for propagating lies (23:13-17).

- After obeying God's mandate to do the painstaking work of writing his prophecies onto a scroll, Jeremiah's work was seized by the king and destroyed. Jeremiah tells us that after each section was read, Jehoiakim would cut the scroll and toss the pieces into the fire. The king's arrogance showed no fear of God and no regard for Jeremiah's labor (36:20-25).

- Ultimately, Jeremiah's final warning against fleeing the land of Israel in fear of Babylonian conquest was rejected, and he was taken against his will to Egypt. Forced to accompany the rebellious leaders of Israel in their act of faithless disobedience, Jeremiah's ministry in the land of promise came to an end through their act of defiance (43:4-7).

- Even in Egypt, under the hand of God's judgment, they would not listen to Jeremiah as he brought God's Word to them and challenged them to repent (44).

From beginning to end, the work of Jeremiah's life was consistently met with rejection and ridicule. There were a few bright spots to be sure, a few times others spoke out in his defense; Baruch his scribe remained faithful, and the remnant in Israel stood firm in their faith. But it was generally a life lived on the roller coaster of discouragement.

Discouragement came to Jeremiah in the course of ministry. It may come your way through any number of vehicles. Regardless of its source, the roller coaster is real, and the turmoil it causes is great.

Discouragement takes its toll. Trite answers are an insult, glibly recited promises slaps in the face. People caught in the ups and downs of discouragement need insights that are tried and true. Solutions that are meaningful must come from the crucible of reality.

MAINTAINING YOUR GRIP

Jeremiah is worth long reflection because the testimony of his life was forged in the crucible of genuine experience. He traveled through the same deep valleys we walk. He is one of those fellow strugglers who has been through the wringer and yet maintained a firm grip on his God. He is well qualified as a mentor and a partner when discouragement seeks to claim us as another victim. He shows us how to maintain a firm grip when life deals its crushing blows.

Woven amidst the content of his messages and the chronicle of his experiences is a powerfully insightful pattern worth following. Jeremiah had a two-fold practice for dealing with the despair of his heart. If you look, you will see it over and over again in both of the books from his pen. He dealt with discouragement two ways:

Tell God the truth about how you feel

and

tell yourself the truth about God.

Sound too simple? It is simple. Why make things harder than they need to be?

#1: Tell God the Truth About How You Feel

Have you ever noticed that the men and women of the Bible often prayed far more gut-wrenchingly honest prayers than we allow ourselves to pray? Their prayers would never pass muster for Sunday school quarterlies. They prayed real-world, emotionally laden prayers of desperation. They minced no words. They pulled no punches. They never prayed to impress. Jeremiah prayed that way. He made it his habit to put all his cards on the table in the course of his prayers.

In his prayer life you see a man who had learned to grab the legs of God's throne and hold on until he knew he had been heard. His were not prayers of defiance, nor demands of a stubborn heart. But he did pray with a brutal honesty that put the matters of his heart clearly in the lap of his God. Even his sternest prayers were never prayed with a clenched fist. They were prayers of a crushed spirit.

People relate to his prayers because of their honesty. They reveal a heart that has been broken on the threshing floor of life. Listen to a few samples.

> *You are always righteous, O LORD,*
> *when I bring a case before you.*
> *Yet I would speak with you about your justice:*
> *Why does the way of the wicked prosper?*
> *Why do all the faithless live at ease?*

(Jeremiah 12:1)

> *O LORD, you deceived me, and I was deceived;*
> *you overpowered me and prevailed.*
> *I am ridiculed all day long; everyone mocks me.*
> *Whenever I speak, I cry out*
> *proclaiming violence and destruction.*
> *So the word of the LORD has brought me*
> *insult and reproach all day long.*

(Jeremiah 20:7-8)

> *Cursed be the day I was born!*
> *May the day my mother bore me not be blessed. . . .*
> *Why did I ever come out of the womb to see*
> *trouble and sorrow*
> *and to end my days in shame?*

(Jeremiah 20:14, 18)

"Look, O LORD, on my affliction, for the
   enemy has triumphed." . . .
"Look, O LORD, and consider, for I am despised.
   Is it nothing to you, all you who pass by?
Look around and see.
   Is any suffering like my suffering that was inflicted on me,
that the LORD brought on me in the day of his fierce anger?
   From on high he sent fire, sent it down into my bones.
He spread a net for my feet and turned me back.
   He made me desolate, faint all the day long."

(Lamentations 1:9, 11-13)

In short, Jeremiah dealt with his despair by taking it *to* the Lord, not *away* from Him. He spoke to his Father in heaven about things as they really were instead of trying to say what he thought God wanted to hear. This is exactly where we need to start.

Prayer is not performance. It is a dynamic encounter between a creature and his Creator. Perhaps the typical prayers of North American saints are less than dynamic because they are less than open. Some folks are afraid that God's first response will be to give out grades on our prayers and then respond based on those grades. Were that the case, most of Jeremiah's prayers would have been failures. His prayers screamed out with real need. They revealed a desperate heart. And as a result they paved the way for God to meet him at precisely his point of need.

Learn from his example. Talk to the Lord about things as you really feel them. Give Him the inside track to the secrets of your heart.

For we do not have a high priest who is unable to
sympathize with our weaknesses, but we have one who has
been tempted in every way, just as we are—yet was without

sin. Let us then approach the throne of grace with
confidence, so that we may receive mercy and find grace to
help us in our time of need.

(Hebrews 4:15-16)

#2: Tell Yourself the Truth About God

The concept of being honest and open with God is easy enough to grasp, even if the practice may take a little getting used to. But our real challenge will be learning to stop and willfully tell ourselves the truth about God. It is this second practice that restores perspective. Jeremiah did not leave the presence of his God without willfully declaring the truth he knew about God.

Do you recall the prayer of Jehoshaphat in 2 Chronicles 20? (See chapter 3 of this book.) Jeremiah adopted a similar pattern. He put as much or more effort into telling himself the truth about God as he did in telling God the truth about himself. When discouraging circumstances cloud your outlook for the moment, review those insights that have guided you in the past.

If you were to look up the full passages from which samples of Jeremiah's prayers were quoted above, you would find something amazing. In every instance, bound together with his bold and truthful declarations of how he feels you will find him reviewing what he knew to be true about God.

In chapter 12 we find:

> *Yet you know me, O LORD;*
> *you see me and test my thoughts about you. (v. 3)*

Sandwiched between his cries in chapter 20 we read:

> *But the LORD is with me like a mighty warrior;*
> *so my persecutors will stumble and not prevail.*

> *They will fail and be thoroughly disgraced;*
>> *their dishonor will never be forgotten.*
> *O LORD Almighty, you who examine the righteous*
>> *and probe the heart and mind,*
> *let me see your vengeance upon them,*
>> *for to you I have committed my cause.*
> *Sing to the LORD!*
>> *Give praise to the LORD!*
> *He rescues the life of the needy*
>> *from the hands of the wicked. (vv. 11-13)*

And in the well-known Lamentations 3 we read:

> *Yet this I call to mind*
>> *and therefore I have hope:*
> *Because of the LORD's great love we are not consumed,*
>> *for his compassions never fail.*
> *They are new every morning; great is your faithfulness.*
>> *I say to myself, " The LORD is my portion;*
> *therefore I will wait for him."*
>> *The LORD is good to those whose hope is in him,*
> *to the one who seeks him;*
>> *it is good to wait quietly*
> *for the salvation of the LORD. (vv. 21-26)*

Jeremiah's prayers were deliberate acts of faith. They were not helpless words thrown into the wind, but honest encounters with the God who reigns beyond the limits of our perspective. Learn from the strength of his testimony. Pray in a way that openly acknowledges the depth of your feelings. Don't sugarcoat your words, but tell God the truth, allowing Him to meet you where you really are. And stay in His presence long enough to deliberately recount what you know to be true about His character and His work.

A SPECIAL WORD FOR THOSE IN MINISTRY

My heart is drawn to speak to pastors and missionaries at this point. The truth is, there are many times when the discouragements of ministry are overwhelming. In fact, everyone who serves in ministry, whether in paid or unpaid positions, encounters seasons of discouragement.

While television and magazines have the ability to create airbrushed images of ministry, real work is done in the trenches. It is characterized more by Paul's "burden for all the churches" than by glitzy campaigns and promotional offers. Most of real ministry is non-glamourous. It happens away from spotlights, during odd hours, and consumes vast quantities of energy.

However, zeal and dedication, faithfulness and hard work do not mean progress will come easily or that culturally defined criteria for success will be the norm. When things aren't happening fast enough, when a church has plateaued or is even declining, when there are few, if any, converts to Christ, when there is resistance or outright rebellion against your ideas, when the efforts for which you have invested so much time and energy are ignored, when problems in your home cloud your joy in ministry, the discouragement can be profound. "After all," it's easy to reason, "we got into this to do something great for God. Why is He letting us down? How can He allow our prayers and sacrifices to count for so little?"

Jeremiah was faithful for forty years. He spoke God's words with conviction and clarity. He never shrank back from opposition. Yet, his experience was one without glamour and without "success" as our culture would define it.

I am sure Jeremiah had days of great encouragement. Days of excitement when God met with him in a special way. Days filled with new methods, new ideas, even new messages from

God. But those days were followed by the downside of the roller coaster—no new results, no new responses.

Everyone I know who serves in ministry is moved by a zeal for the Gospel, a passion to serve God, a commitment to the Scriptures, and a love for people. The very qualities that drive us make us susceptible to the weight of discouragement. Yet, faithful obedience does not always mean impressive results.

Discouragement has a way of causing us to question our calling, to question our involvement, and to question God's desire to use us in any significant way. It doesn't matter whether we serve in the pulpit or in the parking lot, the Sunday school class or the secretary's desk—the issues are the same.

So, stand back and learn from Jeremiah's life. It is clear that he was right where he should have been, doing right what he should be doing, right when he should be doing it. He may have asked some very tough questions, but there is no reason to doubt the essence of his calling or the quality of his ministry.

In your times of discouragement, be slow to deny or forget your own calling from God and His daily presence with you!

KEEP A FULL RESERVOIR

Thinking long-term, you need to build a reservoir of insight into the nature of God and His faithful track record. During times of calm, before you reach the peak and make the plunge, study the Word for insights to carry you through difficult days. During painful days allow the heightened sensitivity brought on by increased need to help you search for sustaining truths in the pages of Scripture. Look for promises and insights you may have missed during calmer days.

- Study the character of God.
- Identify promises of Scripture that touch your spirit, then commit them to memory.

- Make friends with the men and women of Scripture, and let them become your lifelong companions.
- Journal your own experiences of answered prayer and divine guidance. Refer to these during times of despair.
- Keep your eyes open to the handiwork of God in the lives of others. If you cannot see God's handiwork in your life at the moment, watching Him at work in the lives of others can serve as a reminder of His faithful nature and active compassion.

A PERSONAL WORD TO THE DISCOURAGED

Some of you who read this bear the burden of discouragement right now. In a special way I want to exhort you with a few extra comments. Discouragement has a way of sabotaging our faith. It knocks the pilings out from under us and sets us adrift in relentless seas. Left to the limits of our own understanding, we lose sight of God's presence and question His character. That is a lonely place to be. What's worse, our pride makes it hard to let others inside where they might help us carry our burden.

If you are at such a point, my heart is with you. The ache of spirit during times like these seems to know no limit. From personal experience and the testimony of the Scriptures I say to you, don't lose heart. And don't give in to the temptation to work it out alone. If you pull away from God in your pain, the fog of your discouragement will increase the loneliness of your ordeal. Your relationship with your Heavenly Father will be left with a bitter stain that might become permanent. Instead, "Come near to God and he will come near to you" (James 4:8).

Before turning the page, why not engage in a time of brutal openness with your Heavenly Father? Follow the pattern of Jeremiah, and bring your feelings and fears to Him in all their naked ugliness. Don't stop until you have also told yourself the truth about God. Invite Him to sit with you for as long as you are stuck on the roller coaster of discouragement. His compassionate care for you goes far beyond anything you can possibly see at the moment.

THE BOTTOM LINE

The character of God is never synonymous
with the quality of our circumstances. God is good,
even when life stinks.

PART THREE

COMPANIONS ON OUR SEARCH FOR REST

*Because we
need people to walk
beside us*

CHAPTER NINE

When Dreams Hit the Wall

Sarah and Abraham (originally named Sarai and Abram) had long ago given up hope of ever becoming parents. By age sixty-five and seventy-five respectively, they figured the die had been cast. A lifetime of hope lay discarded in the basket of advancing age, leaving little behind but the acrid odor of smoldering dreams.

Comments and questions that had dogged them for decades were rarely noticed any longer. Family functions and whispered glances were by now a familiar piece in the puzzle of childlessness they'd inherited. And as if personal and family disappointment weren't enough, the social climate surrounding them viewed barrenness with disdain. They were objects of suspicion, even viewed by some as cursed by the gods. Hopefully by this stage of life they had learned to accept their lot in life; even so, I doubt if the lonely ache ever really went away.

Until one day.

Out of the blue, one miraculous day it seemed the endless wait would be over.

Abraham was seventy-five years old and was living a prosperous life in the garden city of Haran when God barged in with the dream of a lifetime. In that supernatural encounter God made Abraham a lengthy list of promises. Abraham would become the father of an entire nation. This nation would be as numerous as the stars of the sky and the sand of the sea. And one of his descendants would become God's special instrument of redemption for all mankind. Heady stuff. It was a divine encounter so rich that it still dazzles us 4,000 years later.

There was only one problem. How could Abraham—or anyone—become the father of a multitude when he could not even become the father of one? In their old age, could it really be true? But could it be anything less than true? It was the dream of a lifetime.

I can imagine that for some time after receiving this surprising news Abraham and Sarah walked on clouds of vibrant faith. Without a doubt they told their close friends the great news. Imagine it—after all these years God had promised them a son! This is the kind of news that rekindles romance in a marriage. They were like honeymooners again. For a time the stars looked brighter at night. The odor of their flocks grazing nearby became nostalgic, no longer noxious. Summer wasn't quite so hot. Evening breezes bore a daily aroma of hope and encouragement. It was all too good to believe.

However, euphoria doesn't last long under the heat lamp of time.

And the heat lamp of time burned white-hot, scorching their dreams.

I would guess that initially Sarah counted the days, looking for signs of young life within her aging body. Yet as the months passed, Sarah and Abraham groaned more deeply with each return of her monthly cycle. The childlike faith they'd experienced at first now felt childish. When months became years, tears of disappointment gave way to silent frustration and anger, perhaps even bitterness. Ultimately, ten years passed.

Ten years!

Ten years of waiting. Ten years with no success at becoming pregnant. Ten years of hoping, waiting, giving up, believing, giving up again. Ten years of repetitive questions from well-meaning friends. Ten years with nothing to show for this faith of theirs. After ten years the dream of a son became a nightmare. Hope of a family legacy became a laugh.

Please understand, convictions can be shattered by the incessant pounding of impatience. Rationalization adopts the appearance of logic and dons the look of genuine wisdom. In the quagmire of discouragement, those practices that for years were off-limits and unacceptable look less black and white. The common practices of the world around us can sound like reasonable responses.

Frustrated, confused, Sarah told her husband, "'The LORD has kept me from having children. Go, sleep with my maidservant; perhaps I can build a family through her.' Abram agreed to what Sarai said. . . . He slept with Hagar, and she conceived" (Genesis 16:2).

You can hardly blame them. How many of us could have waited ten years? How many times had they battled with thoughts of this alternative in their minds? How often had they challenged the validity of their convictions? How many of their friends had pushed them with the logic that everyone does it this way? Ultimately they caved in. They took the short-cut, and the consequences were excruciating. Their resistance fell, and great was their pain.

- Sarah lost her friend. Hagar, her longtime friend and handmaiden, became an object of scorn. Hagar, who was once a source of support and assistance, was now a source of ridicule. Hagar, her former confidante, was now an assailant twisting the knife.

- Hagar lost her job and her family. Abraham and Sarah and those who traveled with them were much like an extended family. They had been there for one another through thick and thin in those years of wandering. They provided emotional support for one another. To keep peace with his wife, Abraham sent Hagar and her son away to start a new life.

- Abraham got caught between those he loved. Sarah, his sweetheart of so many years, was now even more heartbroken. Ishmael, the only true son of Abraham's flesh, was forced to leave with Hagar. And on top of it all, Abraham faced the gnawing internal pain that comes from knowing you have only succeeded in making things worse, not better.

The peril of impatience rose again. (See the lessons of chapter 6.) From our vantage point and our ability to read the entire account of those long, dry years in a few minutes, it's easy to miss the day in and day out reality of their experience. It's easy to miss the fact that in Abraham and Sarah we have two friends with whom we can relate when our own dreams hit the wall.

WHEN IT'S YOUR TURN

We'll come back to Abraham and Sarah in a moment, but this is a good place to stop and think through the connection more closely. Each of us has hopes and dreams for our lives. While we may not have received them via middle-of-the-night divine intervention, they are some of the most intimate and important aspects of our lives. We hold them close to the vest, usually revealing them to very few others. And when they hit the wall, when the prospects of seeing them fulfilled go from dim to nonexistent, we wrestle with some of the harshest disappointment in all of life. Dreams die hard and pull our spirits down as they go.

When our dreams hit the wall, we feel alone. We ponder embarrassing and impolite questions about God and His work. It is easy to lose hope, to feel betrayed and abandoned, to wonder if God is angry with us or is punishing us for some reason. We ask an endless stream of questions—the kind that have no answers.

When dreams die, or when they appear to, the ensuing disappointment makes us feel as if God has betrayed our faith. It's a crash-and-burn experience that drives us from the heights to the depths emotionally. We feel the overpowering desire to do something, to do *anything*, to find some way to gain a little bit of control. If you've been there, it's easier to understand the situation Sarah and Abraham faced and the mental gymnastics that made the action with Hagar seem plausible. If only they had known the end from the beginning, perhaps they could have bypassed the consequences of their compromise. Then again, if only we could see our own circumstances that clearly . . .

What are your dreams? How alive are they at the moment? Is there some wall in the present or in the near future against which they'll crash? And perhaps most importantly, how is the process affecting your relationship with God? When dreams die, that hurts.

Maybe your dream is as commonplace as owning your own home, but job status, inflation, family crisis, or something else is standing in the way. Maybe you have dreams about your retirement years, but changes in your community or in national economics have derailed those plans and left you with few desirable alternatives. Perhaps you have hopes and dreams for your career, but now you find yourself shoved to the sidelines of your career path.

Although it is not the hot-button of this decade, midlife crises are often brutally painful journeys through this very battlefield. Somewhere during the middle years of life most of us wrestle with the contrast of our day-to-day experiences versus the dreams of our youth. It becomes apparent that we will not become all we wanted to be. We won't be able to do all we wanted to do. The legacy and accomplishments we'd hoped to leave behind seem beyond our reach. Perhaps, like Abraham, we really blew it somewhere along the way, or perhaps we are affected by circumstances that are no fault of our own. There is no way out, no way to reverse the clock, no way to undo what's been done.

Pastors, missionaries, and others who have devoted their lives to ministry, whether in paid or volunteer positions, find their dreams often hit the wall, too.

Our church supports a missionary couple who are involved in Bible translation. They were called to the mission field as a second career and have given up the luxuries of life that would have been theirs had they stayed put. However, six to seven years into their work, the country where they had gone required most missionaries to leave. With sadness Ted and Kris moved back to the States and adjusted to carrying on their work long-distance. It was harder and slower, but they kept at it.

Twenty years later and with the final stretch in sight, Ted contracted leukemia. *Crash!* Their dream, their life's work, their passion for bringing the Word of God to the people they loved— it all hit the wall. The dream, the work of their lives, was within reach, and now this!

Scared but determined, they didn't give up. Rather, they marched forward through chemotherapy and the energy-draining process that goes along with treatment, all the while putting in as many hours of work as they could physically manage. With an uncertain future and no miraculous promises unveiled by visions in the night, they hung in there, committed to the eternal work carried out by the Spirit of God through His Word.

The chemo was successful, and Ted's leukemia went into remission. Work resumed full steam ahead. Now, over twenty-two years after they began, the New Testament is heading to the printers. (It will come off the presses about the same time as this book.) Yet, even so, there are very few converts in the target village about which they can brag to supporting churches back home.

I have tremendous respect for the integrity and faithfulness of Ted and Kris over these two decades and for thousands of others just like them. I know there have been days when it seemed like their hopes and dreams, their calling from God, were trapped against a wall with no solution to be found. Yet, they have not given up. They continue to do what they know God has called them to do. In spite of personal feelings and times of discouragement, they keep on and entrust the passion of their dreams into the arms of God's grace. They have waited on the Lord and have allowed Him to take care of things in His time and in His way.

Everyone who finds the substance of their dreams smoldering in the wastebasket wrestles with a flood of emotions and unnerving questions. We long for logical answers and rational explanations even when we know that the best of explanations will not be enough to soothe our emotions. In those moments we need people. We need companions who have been there and made it through to the other side. We need partners who can remind us of God's faithfulness when we can't see it on our own. We need people like Abraham to bring us hope and understanding.

Knowing that we would need companions like Abraham, the Spirit of God has preserved many details of his life. And even more importantly, in so doing He has made it clear that God understands how we feel when our own dreams hit the wall. We know there is no magic solution to make everything better, but we need to know God is with us. The story of Abraham serves as a reminder that God never abandons us even when the pressures of time tempt us to believe otherwise. Even when God seems silent, the truth is, He understands how we feel and remains actively involved in our lives.

BACK TO THE DRAWING BOARD

Genesis 16 ends with these words: "Abram was eighty-six years old when Hagar bore him Ishmael." Genesis 17 begins with these words: "When Abram was ninety-nine years old . . ."

If we thought that ten years of waiting, hoping, and dreaming was long, during the breath between the sentence that completes chapter 16 and the one that begins chapter 17, thirteen more years elapse without any further recorded contact from God. Thirteen extra years of waiting and wondering while Abraham's aging body relegated his dream of a son to a memory of the past.

All together, twenty-five years passed between the first word of promise and the arrival of the son of promise. Abraham first heard God's promises in a dream at age seventy-five. Isaac was born to him at age one hundred. Twenty-five years of delay in the Refiner's fire. Can you even imagine what it must have been like to wonder and wait that long?

Having thought at length about the personal trauma of Abraham and Sarah's experience, try to imagine yourself suggesting to them some of the trite advice we've heard so often:

"Have you two prayed about it? Maybe God doesn't want you to have children."

"If only you had more faith, God could perform a miracle."

"Perhaps there is unconfessed sin in your life. If you would repent of it, then God would be free to pour His blessing upon you."

"How can you be sure that the vision you had came from the Lord? What if it was just wishful thinking, a self-fulfilling prophecy of some sort? You just saw and heard what you wanted to hear."

"It's OK—you should rejoice. It's obvious that God has something better in mind for you! After all, all things work together for good."

Comments like these are shared frequently between well-intentioned friends. Yet, they all seem to assume that if we just do the right thing, whatever that is, we will force God to do what we want.

Of course, Abraham and Sarah prayed about their situation. I'm certain that on more than one occasion they searched their hearts and wrestled with the quality of their faith. They probably even tried negotiating with God, just like we do so often today. I am sure they tried everything they could think of to speed the process along. But in the end they were pilgrims traveling through one of life's valleys, and there was no way out. Not until the timing of God was perfect.

There is no hint in Scripture that God was angry over something in their lives. There is no criticism of their attitudes. In fact, in light of the fact that Abraham is the consummate model of living by faith, it would seem that God was well-pleased with them. Were they perfect? No, of course not. But did their imperfections have anything to do with the delayed fulfillment of their dreams? No.

So often we attempt to negotiate with God. We'll even agree to our circumstances as they are in the hope that then God will change them to what we wish they were. We act as if there is something inherently wrong with being stuck in the valley of broken dreams. Yet, it seems that for most of us, just as for Abraham, that is exactly the place where God wants us to be. As hard as it may be at times, the valley of broken dreams is also a place of accelerated growth. The soil there nurtures the richest fruit.

FRUIT FROM THE ASHES

A number of things happen to us during those long seasons when dreams lay dashed against the wall. These are not easy lessons, but they are made of pure gold. They are lessons of the sort that we profoundly admire in others, though they come through a more difficult and more painful process than we like to admit. There are no shortcuts.

Brokenness may be the greatest lesson learned during this process. Brokenness is that ability to stand before God and others openhanded—no longer preoccupied with yourself, your abilities, or your dreams for life. Broken people have stopped making demands about how or when things should happen. They have stopped bragging or dreaming about how much they might do for God. Instead, they stand available for God to do anything He pleases. They have discovered that everything of significance begins and ends with Him. Broken people have discovered a level of dependency on the Spirit of God that causes every step to be one of intimacy and privilege. And quite often they have found that the path to brokenness began when their dreams were shattered.

A revealing moment occurred when Abraham was ninety-nine years old. This incident offers a fascinating glimpse into the work God had done in Abraham's life during twenty-four years of waiting. One day the Lord appeared to Abraham again, and in the process of giving him and his wife new names, names befitting the promise, God also reaffirmed the promise of a son.

You would think that after twenty-four years this moment would elicit overwhelming joy. After years of silence and uncertainty this message should have brought out a few hallelujahs. But Abraham says something entirely different. In effect he said, "Sarah and I are both old now. We are content with the way things are. Perhaps you could channel the promise through Ishmael. Let him live under Your blessing. We harbor no ill will over this delay and would be content with these alternate plans. Lord, we let go of our dreams years ago, and we are at peace about it." (I believe this is the subtext behind Genesis 18:18.)

Abraham had given up any demand that God fulfill his dream the way he had wanted it fulfilled. He had been broken of any drive to make it happen using his own methods. After all the years of disappointment and frustration, wanting to make it happen at any cost, Abraham had stopped making demands. He felt no betrayal by God but rather was at rest. He had learned to trust the Lord even when things happen differently than expected.

"Lord, my dream was for a son through Sarah, an Isaac of our own. But You are free to do things any way You like."

When our dreams hit the wall, quite often God is asking us to give them up. Not give them up superficially so that we might get what we want through some other means, but give them up with an understanding that the dreams aren't coming back. Letting go of our dreams means our future will not be the way we always expected. Only then, when we have released our death grip on what we believe God should do, the way we believe He should do it, and when we believe it should happen, are we free to fully receive whatever He has for us.

Abraham was a different man at 100 than he was at seventy-five. In fact, he was so profoundly changed by God's plans for his life that a few years later he was willing to sacrifice his dream on a makeshift altar. He was willing to give up the son of promise, knowing that the God of the promise could be trusted for more than Abraham could see.

Fruit grows out of the ashes of broken dreams. There are lessons for this life and eternal rewards for the next. The journey is anything but easy and offers very few similarities to our own timetables. Yet through it all, do not mistake the difficulty of the journey for the absence of God's compassionate and faithful handiwork. He is there, whether you can see Him or not.

THE BOTTOM LINE

> Far from being a sign of disapproval, seasons of silence
> may even be indicators of God's pleasure.

A GENTLE WORD OF CAUTION . . .

I would like to express an additional concern here. To put it bluntly, many of our dreams are self-centered and ego-driven. We want possessions and positions that will make us look good or provide greater comfort. These are not always blatant and bold wishes, but the drives behind them can be off the mark. For instance, perhaps we really long for a career jump so we can make more money, buy a bigger house or a more expensive car, or travel to more exotic destinations.

Sounds a little earthy in black and white, doesn't it? And perhaps the picture doesn't fit you. But please read on. You may achieve some or all of these wishes; if so, praise the Lord. But on the other hand, keep James 4:3 in mind: "When you ask, you do not receive, because you ask with wrong motives, that you may spend what you get on your pleasures." Your dream for some of these things may hit the wall because God knows what is best for you. He will not nurture motives or desires out of line with His agenda.

So, the question facing us is still the same: are we willing to trust God enough to let Him have His way when His way is different than our own? Are we willing to let Him have our dreams so that He can let us have what is best from an eternal perspective? It may very well be that having our dreams fulfilled the way we envision would be the absolute worst thing that could happen to us.

If God calls you to put your dreams on the altar, trust Him to replace them or revive them in a way that makes the original pale by comparison.

CHAPTER TEN

Stuck on Hold

It used to be that if you called someone and found yourself placed on hold, you stayed in limbo with nothing to do but listen to electronic gurgles within the phone system. These days, once you have touch-toned your way past a computerized options menu, you at least have some easy-listening music to occupy your attention. But let me ask you, do you feel any differently about sitting there on hold? Being put on hold in any situation is something we detest.

A few years ago I was on a flight to Denver that was assigned to an indefinite holding pattern because of weather-caused delays at the airport. Not an uncommon experience, but still an irritating one. Air travel is convenient and in general fairly comfortable, but a few hours in those cramped seats breathing stale, mechanically-filtered air takes its toll. A person's body is eager to get up, stretch, and move freely again.

When it's time for a flight, you mentally prepare yourself for a few hours of confinement, knowing that it gets you where you need to go and that once there you will be rewarded with freedom again. And besides, if the flight is fairly smooth, you'll be able to catch up on some reading, get some work done, rest a little, or perhaps do a bit of all three. My flight to Denver had already afforded enough time to complete the things I had brought with me to get done.

Just about the time my feet were getting antsy and my internal alarm announced that we should be starting our descent sometime soon, the pilot's voice came over the air. "Good afternoon, ladies and gentlemen, this is the captain speaking. Weather conditions have restricted landings at Stapleton Airport, and we have entered a holding pattern. I'll keep you posted as soon as I have any further information. In the meantime, just sit back and relax. Our flight crew will be happy to assist you in any way they can."

Sit back and relax? I was tired of sitting back and relaxing. I wanted to be standing and walking—off the airplane, through the terminal, and into the car that would take me downtown for the meeting that had brought me here. So much for what I had planned. Instead, there we were, flying circles at 15- or 20,000 feet somewhere over the northern plains states. Oh well, how long could this last anyway?

As we flew past the sixty minute mark in our subsonic holding pattern, the natives started getting restless. Most of us had business to be conducted, people who were waiting for or depending on us, meetings to be attended or led, or vacation time to be enjoyed. None of us wanted to be where we were. And none of us could do anything about it.

Somewhere around the ninety minute mark the pilot came back on the PA to announce that things were improving slightly in Denver, and if we were lucky we might get a landing slot. However, if nothing opened up for us soon, fuel consumption would force us to land at some other airport, whereupon the airline would bus us back to Denver.

Oh great! First we miss our afternoon engagements, and then we find out that we may not be able to land in Denver at all. And what is this about running low on fuel? It is not very comforting to find yourself flying in an aluminum tube at 20,000 feet with little fuel and prowling around the country for another airport that may or may not allow you to land, knowing that even if you succeed in that mission you'll have to board a bus and drive who knows how many hours through a snowstorm back to the city where you should have been hours ago.

Nothing is quite like having your plans and schedule put on hold with no means to do anything about it.

Ever been in a similar situation? Sure, you have. Someone or something threw a wrench into the works, and all of your plans went out the window. You were put on hold. Stuck in traffic. Held up from completing a project because of someone else's failure to complete their assignment. Shut out of an opportunity because of a message lost, a phone call missed, or a snafu with the mail. You've been stuck on hold, and it is frustrating to say the least!

But what about those times when your life is put on hold in a really big way? Phone calls, delayed flights, traffic jams—these are small potatoes, really. My flight eventually did land in Denver a couple of hours later than originally scheduled, but one lost afternoon is nothing compared to those seasons of life when your whole life has been put on hold. Considering we have such a struggle over the small stuff, how in the world do we cope with the big stuff?

For instance, a friend of mine has lived the past five years with his career on hold. He is in a field he enjoys and is highly skilled in certain areas. However, the demand for his expertise is diminishing at a steady rate as a result of changes in his industry. Not to be foolish, my friend has sought out training and experience in other related areas, seeking to branch out, expand his skill base, and make himself marketable as an individual with multifaceted abilities.

A man who loves the Lord Jesus Christ and seeks to be obedient to Him, this friend of mine struggles intensely with private questions and fears about what God is doing—or not doing. It seems as if his life has been put on hold. The future is unclear, the present is unpredictable, and the direction he should take uncertain.

Stuck on hold.

We all feel stuck on hold during those times when, through no fault of our own, we are bogged down in circumstances that derail our plans. Times when the next steps are out of our control. Times when we really need to wait on the Lord, but His presence and involvement are hard to discern. Times when God is silent and the rest of life bears down on us, demanding that we take action.

If you haven't encountered times like this, you might be the lone exception. They are a common experience. Yet, despite the fact that all of us encounter seasons of life when we feel put on hold, when it happens we feel unusually alone. This on-hold feeling is tough to describe and thus difficult to share with others. Worse, it doesn't fit our expectations of how God should work, and so addressing Him becomes difficult as well.

It is time to be reintroduced to an old friend—to look closely at the story of his life and discover a companion on our journey. His testimony will be encouraging, but even more, there is a legacy of his life that you can draw upon. His legacy will prove to be a treasure chest of tools and insights you can use to guide you through those seasons when you feel left on hold.

This old friend? David.

He makes a great companion because he endured years and years of life stuck on hold. Through the infallible inspiration of the Spirit of God, we have a trustworthy account of his life available for our study. We not only have a reliable picture of those on-hold years, but we have an even greater resource in the written fruit of those years—the Psalms.

Seeing the familiar with fresh eyes can be a difficult challenge, but I ask you to try. The more you understand the dynamics of David's years in limbo, the more you will appreciate the wealth of his legacy in the Psalms. And the more you are able to recognize the Psalms as David's survival tools, the more you will be able to draw upon them in your own life.

Join me for a walk through the on-hold years of David's life. Allow yourself a little sanctified imagination, and try to picture yourself walking in his shoes. Try to imagine how he must have felt, how the circumstances must have looked, how ravenously he must have searched for answers. All the while, keep in mind that in spite of the stress-filled and frightening experiences he faced, David emerged as a man after God's own heart.

We'll outline his experience by citing the types of responses we express during those days when life puts us on hold.

RESPONSE #1: "I DIDN'T ASK FOR THIS"

It all started one day while David was out shepherding the family flocks. Actually it had started earlier during Samuel's final encounter with Saul; but David was unaware of that encounter or the outcome of it. Unaware until now, that is. Right in the middle of the lazy part of the afternoon, a messenger arrived demanding that David return home for some sort of urgent family business.

Any good shepherd hesitates to leave his flock in the care of another, but if it was urgent, who could refuse? Nothing major had happened, he hoped, no family crisis. After all, his brothers were temporarily home from warring against the Philistines, and his father was in great health. What could it be?

Seeing the prophet Samuel in his home was an honor David had never imagined. What would he, God's revered spokesman, want to say to or do with the family of Jesse? David bowed slightly in respect for this great man and out of honor for the God they both loved. And then the strangest thing started happening.

No one in the house seemed quite ready for this, but as David bowed, Samuel stood and embraced him. He said something about a king that no one quite understood and then reached into his pocket for a small horn of oil.

Then, in the presence of David's father and brothers, Samuel began delicately pouring the oil over David's head. Placing his hands upon the shepherd lad's head and shoulders, Samuel announced that God had chosen him to be the new king of Israel. He pronounced a blessing over David and prayed the kind of moving prayers that only a man of profound wisdom and experience knows how to pray. No one else said a word. No one dared pose a question, although older brothers always find jealousy impossible to escape in a moment like this. As Samuel stood among them that day, the Spirit of God settled on that place, and everyone knew this was right. Then the prophet left.

From David's experience, it all happened too fast, coming out of the blue. No warning. No time to adjust. No time to call friends and relatives to witness this momentous occasion. Things like this don't happen to youngest brothers. And they don't come unannounced—or do they?

What followed this moment of divine intervention and supernatural career planning?

Nothing!

By all appearances once Samuel left, life in Jesse's household returned to normal. The brothers returned to Saul's side as soldiers, and David returned to his role among the sheep. There was no throne, no national press release, no plans for an inauguration, no return visits from Samuel—nothing! And this delay was no small thing! Although David had been anointed king, he was not appointed to the throne until he was twenty-three years old. And he did not rule as king over all of Israel until he was thirty years old. He was stuck for years, waiting for the fulfillment of the promise. The king-to-be was on indefinite hold.

Let's dig into this timetable thing a bit further. We know how old he was when he became king over Judah (twenty-three) and over all of Israel (thirty), but we don't have an exact age for when he was anointed.

We do know that he was the youngest of eight brothers. We also know that he was too young to fight in Saul's army. We know that the ongoing war with the Philistines demanded a standing army Saul was forever trying to strengthen. First Samuel 14:52 says that "whenever Saul saw a mighty or brave man, he took him into service." We know David was both mighty and brave; so our only conclusion must be that he was too young. Could we say somewhere around fifteen years of age? If he'd been much older, he would have been drafted.

Whether he was older or younger by a little, the point is still the same. From the time David was anointed as the king over Israel until the time he actually began to reign as king was in the ballpark of fifteen years! At the very least, it was seven or eight years until he was allowed to reign over the one tribe of Judah!

How long have you been required to wait? How long has your future been on hold? David never asked to be king. He wasn't campaigning. He was minding his own business when God intervened and sent him on this path of interminable delay.

RESPONSE #2: "NOTHING I DO MATTERS"

What follows Samuel's dramatic intervention in David's life is a series of simple acts whereby David unassumingly demonstrated his worthiness for the position.

His first assignment was to minister to Saul with his music. This is an odd challenge. Saul was losing his mind, and David was sent to help him regain it. Or to say it differently, David was sent to make it possible for the one who stood in his way to stand in his way even longer.

His encounter with Goliath was the second public assignment on his path to the palace.

You know the story. One large, ugly Philistine made the entire army of Israel run to their tents quaking in their boots. And he did it twice a day for forty days in a row! The best Israel could do was muster up a little locker-room bravado over breakfast, far away from the gaze of Goliath. Then in walked David with snacks for his brothers and with the assignment to bring home news about their well-being.

Embarrassed at the lack of faith shown by his countrymen and outraged over the accusations made by this arrogant superhero against his God, David volunteered to take matters into his own hands. The rest is history.

Now people began to take notice of this shepherd boy from Judah, and they began to compose ballads about his conquests. Additionally, his assorted victories over the Philistines brought national acclaim and the growing recognition that this was God's anointed. But to what end?

The more David did what was right in service to his country and to Saul his king, the more Saul was irked. Before long, Saul began initiating efforts to take David's life. Nothing David did had any apparent effect on moving him closer to the palace. Nothing made any difference in helping him take his rightful place on the throne.

So often it is the same for us. When our lives have been placed on hold, it seems that nothing we do makes a difference toward improving our circumstances.

RESPONSE #3: "WHAT DIFFERENCE DOES OBEDIENCE MAKE?"

Obedience to the Lord is always right. Choosing the godly option is always the right choice. Unfortunately, during those stuck-on-hold times it is tempting to believe that obedience is a means of obligating God to act according to our expectations. It isn't. It is also easy to rationalize compromising our behavior when nothing we do makes a difference in our predicament.

That is one of the things that impresses me about David. When you look at Saul's ungodly behavior, at his brazen attempts to kill David, at his cold-blooded murder of the priests at Nob, and at two opportunities when God placed Saul right in David's hands, it is easy to imagine David justifying a course of action for himself as God's supposed instrument of justice and judgment. He didn't. He continued to live in obedience and to wait for God to execute His perfect timing in His perfect way, no matter how long it took.

The longer the wait, the easier it is to rationalize our behavior. When obedience doesn't bring about a desired change, it is tempting to give up. You know the temptation. So did David. Yet somehow he resisted the lure of the quick fix. His obedience appeared fruitless for a time, but the truth is that it was his commitment to obedience and godliness in spite of circumstances that made David the influential leader he was.

Keep your guard up. When you find yourself thinking that your behavior doesn't matter, recognize that it does. When obedience seems to make no difference, refuse to believe it. Your behavior matters whether you see the outcome of it or not!

RESPONSE #4: "THAT'S THE FINAL STRAW"

David had held on for years. Saul was fighting against him, but in the back of his mind David knew Samuel would be there when the time came to set things right. Samuel would speak for God and erase any confusion among the people. The memory of that day—of the oil running down his forehead, of Samuel's hands upon his shoulders, the words of blessing David had heard spoken—kept David going and hoping. Samuel would vouch for David at the right time, in God's perfect time.

Then Samuel died.

Now what! Saul was determined to murder David and so eradicate this threat to his kingdom rule. Popular support for David was strong, but popular support is always fickle.

Now Samuel would not be there for David in the future as he'd hoped. David must have been crushed. He might have been afraid. The internal impact on David might explain why he fled to the desert of Maon immediately following the burial of Samuel. He moved as far away from Saul as he could get.

Samuel's death parallels the last-straw feeling that usually accompanies helpless situations we encounter. For a while, no matter how bleak things look, there is usually some glimmer of hope provided by someone or something. But sooner or later that final glimmer is extinguished. What happens then? Often we crash and burn. Discouragement floods in, and our faith falters.

In those moments we feel as if the rope has been cut, and we are sent into a free fall without hope. Those are dark days. Days that demand that we recognize an important truth: from the beginning our hope was never in the strength of that last straw. Samuel was never the guarantee of David's future. Samuel was merely a spokesman for God's perfect plans. His death was a loss, but it didn't change the situation one iota. It is the same with the loss of your Samuel. In truth, God has been your only hope all along.

RESPONSE #5: "HOW LONG CAN THIS GO ON, LORD?"

At some point during those days when we seem to be stuck on hold, fatigue takes over. Gone are logical arguments with God about how or why circumstances should be better than they are. Gone are reasons for and anticipation of change. In their place fatigue speaks out with the simplest of all questions: "How much longer can this go on, Lord?"

Late-night conversations between David and his Lord must have included questions of weariness. "How many more cold, desert nights will I be stuck out here? How many more days will my men and I spend on the run, hungry and exhausted, with inadequate food supplies? How many more close calls with Saul will I be forced to endure? How much longer, Lord?"

In those days when you reach the dregs of fatigue, consider this: the passing of time is only a crisis on *our* calendar, never on God's. He who never slumbers and never grows weary is at work not only in our circumstances but in our hearts during the very days when weariness is at its greatest. Those days are never wasted and never for naught.

A LEGACY OF HOPE

Out of the well of David's experience comes a fountain of riches for us. The lessons he learned, the meditations of his heart that renewed his spirit, and the chronicle of his prayers were written as poetry and recorded in the songbook of the Scriptures.

For thousands of years the people of God have gone to the songs of David and others. The Psalms have been the hymnbook of the faithful since the compositions of Moses were first sung in the desert. The Psalms have a way of shaping and guiding our prayers. They have a way of redirecting the attitude of our hearts. They bring hope to the grieving, strength to the weary, and a higher perspective to the discouraged. It's no wonder we love those poems.

The Psalms are a treasure chest to be opened and cherished. When your life is on hold, wade through their familiar pages; allow their words to shape your prayers when you have no words of your own. Allow the Psalms to become your close companions when you have no clue regarding God's agenda for your life. They are tried and true and preserved for you by the compassionate work of the very God who walks with you, even through the valley of the shadow of death.

As you dwell in the Psalms, take notice of those written by David. David, the shepherd. David, the military genius. David, the king. David, the musician. David, the man after God's own heart. Ask yourself why David was so capable of composing psalms to which we can relate so deeply. Stop to consider the circumstances of his life that gave birth to such emotionally raw and spiritually uplifting songs.

This man after God's own heart, who spent so many years in the public spotlight, began in the darkness of uncertainty. Yet, during those very years of delay many of the Psalms were written. Seventy-three of the Psalms are ascribed to David, and of those, thirteen identify the historical context during which they were written. Of those thirteen, every one was written in a period of difficulty, and at least seven were written during the on-hold years between David's anointing and his actual ascension to the throne. His tenderness toward God, his raw and honest prayer life, his grasp of the character of God, and his willingness to trust in God's timing no matter how things looked were all born in adversity.

When you find yourself immersed in circumstances that try your faith and crush your spirit, recognize that it was just such adversity that became the Master Jeweler's tools to craft spiritual treasure in David's life. The influence of his life that still touches us today is the product of God's craftsmanship during the years when his future seemed on hold and circumstances made no sense.

THE BOTTOM LINE

God loves us too much to take anything less than
an aggressive role in the development of our character.

CHAPTER ELEVEN

When God Seems to Have Forgotten

Consider this simple truth: there are times when life is unfair. Times when someone else's ill-advised decisions wreak havoc on our lives. Times when someone else's clearly sinful behavior collides with our plans, our hopes, and our future. Times when the emotional fallout of undesirable circumstances causes us to toy with doubts about the level of God's concern. And if these conditions persist, they form a breeding ground for the quiet, bitter suspicion that God may not care as much as we thought He did. Painfully, these times of lingering difficulty may lead us to feel forgotten.

Granted, the overwhelming testimony of Scripture is that God is fully aware of what His children are facing and is actively concerned for their welfare. He who holds the universe together by the power of His word, who does not sleep and never grows weary, is never caught by surprise and can never forget His children. Psalm 139 and other Bible passages tell us that we are never without His presence and intimate involvement. But regardless, on an emotional level there are times when we cannot reconcile the promises of Scripture with the experience of our circumstances.

In the darkness of those days we cry out, "Where are You God? What are You doing?"

> How long, O LORD? Will you forget me forever? How long will you hide your face from me? How long must I wrestle with my thoughts and every day have sorrow in my heart? How long will my enemy triumph over me? Look on me and answer, O LORD my God. Give light to my eyes, or I will sleep in death.

> (Psalm 13:1-3)

I want to introduce you to another companion for the difficult days of your journey. You know him already, but perhaps not in this light. His name is Joseph, and the testimony of his life is a clear example of God's work outside the veil of our understanding. His story empathizes with our disappointments and offers us hope.

Since the details of Joseph's life are probably familiar to you, I challenge you to slow down and discover the nuances of his daily experience. (We will be skimming through the account of Joseph's life on the assumption that you recall its basic outline. However, if your memory of the events of his life is not fresh, I suggest that you complement your reading of this chapter by reading the biblical account in Genesis 37–50.) Linger with me now at some of the moments in his life when he could have justifiably cried out, "Where are You God? What are You doing?"

To be fair to the biblical record, you need to know that in the account of his life there are no questions of doubt recorded. But we know how he felt about the cards he was dealt. He classified his brothers' heartless betrayal as "evil" (Genesis 50:20, KJV), and he described his own life as a sojourn through "the land of my suffering" (Genesis 41:52). In short, while we do not have a detailed report of his feelings, we do have a summary. We also know enough details to intelligently imagine what it must have been like for him. Let's take what we know and consider the kinds of questions he might have asked at each turn of events.

THE HIJACKING OF HIS FUTURE

You know about the conspiracy of Joseph's brothers, but have you ever stopped to wonder about the unwritten aspects of that event? For instance, had the brothers ever made private threats to Joseph in their jealous mania? When Joseph was traveling the sixty miles to find his brothers and the family flocks, did he have any anxiety over their reception in an area without witnesses? When he was thrown down that empty well by his brothers, was he injured by the fall? Was he able to hear their discussions as they debated his future? How long was he abandoned to the echo of his own fears at the bottom of that dark cistern? When they lowered a rope and pulled him out, was he prepared for their verdict?

Sold to Midianite traders so they could in turn sell him as a slave to some Egyptian—what a nightmare! What about his father? How would the brothers explain this to him? Would they tell some lie about Joseph's death? There would be no hope of ever seeing him again. Joseph wouldn't even have a chance to say goodbye.

Can you imagine the whirlwind of thoughts racing through Joseph's mind during the days he traveled with the Midianites to Egypt? Helpless to do anything and securely bound lest this newly acquired investment try to escape, Joseph was trapped. His future thrown away. No one would search for him. No one would come to rescue him. The situation was irreversible, and his feelings were irrelevant. He was alone. Abandoned. At the mercy of people whom he did not know, men who had no fear of God. Where was God? What was He doing ? Why would He allow something like this to happen?

The account of this life-changing episode in Joseph's life is contained within a few verses of Scripture. Yet, beneath the surface it is easy to see a whole range of human emotions and concerns that were undoubtedly present. As we consider the life of Joseph, and as you study Scripture on your own, be careful of two factors that can diminish the impact of the holy record. First, we can read in moments what covered days, months, even years in someone's life. So, consciously slow down and look for hints at the human experience beneath and between the words of Scripture.

The second factor to overcome is our familiarity with the passages. Because we are familiar with Joseph's whole story, it is easy to view each development in light of how it all ends. However, when we do that, we miss what it was like for him. He had no idea what would be the outcome of any steps in his journey. He only knew what was happening at the moment. He could only make the decisions at hand. He could only trust God by faith. He had no clue what would happen years later. His experience was exactly like our own from day to day. We can only see and deal with the cards we've been dealt today. We press forward by faith alone, never certain of what lies down the road. At the end of the road we are confident of heaven, but between then and now we can only take one step at a time.

SLAVE TO AN EXECUTIONER

Arriving in Egypt as a piece of human cargo, Joseph had a whole new basket of concerns. He was in a strange land populated by a strange people. He knew no one; he had no rights and no control over his future. Who would purchase him? What kind of work would he be required to do? What if Pharaoh bought him to work on one of those physically crushing building programs? What would the meat rack of the slave auction be like?

Then it was done. He had been purchased by some high-ranking Egyptian official named Potiphar. Language differences made it difficult to communicate very well at first, but something about the man's dress, his entourage, and the authority of his stride told Joseph that this was a man to be feared.

Imagine how Joseph felt when he discovered that his new master was the captain of Pharaoh's bodyguards, the chief executioner of Egypt! He had been sold as a slave to the deadliest man in the land. This man would have the authority to take Joseph's life with the slightest provocation. What hope was there for the future now? "Lord, where are You in all of this? What are You doing?"

Joseph's only option was to work hard and live as a man of integrity. That is, to live in such a way that he could live with himself. But during the months and years that followed in Potiphar's house, nothing would change the fact that he was a slave. Nothing could change the fact that he lived in Egypt separated from his family, with no control of his future. Alone and forgotten.

BURNED BY A SECOND COAT

Potiphar recognized something unique about Joseph. Everyone did. No matter where he worked, no matter what responsibility he was given, no matter how challenging the task, prosperity reigned. Joseph possessed a genuine Midas touch. But it was more than that. Potiphar demanded hard work and excellence of all his slaves—it was what he was used to. But in Joseph there was something extra. The Lord was behind Joseph's success, blessing everything he touched. Over time as Joseph's integrity proved as true as the Lord's blessing, he was appointed CEO of Potiphar, Inc.

It's a classic rags-to-riches story that even begins with family intrigue. A seventeen-year-old boy is kidnapped and sold into slavery in a foreign country. There, as a slave, he works hard, proves his worth, and climbs to the top, eventually running the empire of one of Egypt's most powerful men. Inspirational. The kind of story that ends with everyone living happily ever after. The only problem is, it didn't work out that way.

When we read this part of the story, it's easy to miss the fact that even in this position of success Joseph was still a slave in a foreign land, with no hope of ever being reunited with his family. Do you think he ever gave up dreaming about his homeland? Did he ever spend a lonely evening longing for the familiar foods and music of his people? Could anything truly fill the ache for home and family?

At least life in Potiphar's house was pleasant and predictable. It gave Joseph a chance to consider the future again. It was different than the future he dreamed of as a boy, but it wasn't so bad here. If he continued to work hard and honor the wishes of his master, life could be good.

Life in Egypt might have been good for Joseph had Potiphar's wife not derailed his life. Unjustly accused, humiliated when he had acted with integrity, imprisoned indefinitely, for the second time Joseph was betrayed by someone close to him.

You could argue that at least he was alive. True. In fact, it is possible that Joseph's life was spared because Potiphar doubted his wife's tale. Prison was a way for Potiphar to save face and spare Joseph's life at the same time. Whatever the reasons, Joseph was now in prison, the place of ultimate helplessness, facing an eternity of monotony. Familiar questions quickly raged anew. "Where are You in all of this, God? Why are You allowing Your servant to be unjustly imprisoned? How can I serve You here?"

PROMISES, PROMISES, PROMISES

Genesis 39 concludes by describing Joseph's situation in prison. Then chapter 40 begins with these ominous words: "Some time later . . ." The words just hang there. They bring us face to face with the great test of prison life: time.

No specific quantity to be measured. No milestones to be counted. An endless succession of days. An endless repetition of routines. For people whose lives have been derailed, it seems that time always passes like this—one day after another without news, without progress, without change—a relentless blur of time. "Some time later . . ."

I wish we knew exactly how much time went by while Joseph was there in prison.

We know that he was seventeen when his brothers abducted him (Genesis 37:2). And we know that he was thirty years old when he was appointed to serve alongside Pharaoh (Genesis 41:46). Between those two dates he served a stint in Potiphar's house and "some time" here in prison. If by some chance the years were equally divided between the two, it would mean he spent over six years in prison. Perhaps it was longer, perhaps shorter. Either way, we know it was a matter of years, because of what is recorded next in Genesis 40.

One day out of the blue there came a glimmer of hope. While in prison, paying the penalty for a king's tantrum, Pharaoh's baker and cupbearer had dreams they couldn't understand. Now it just so happened that they had been assigned to Joseph's care while in prison. Clever of God, don't you think?

Joseph's interpretation of their dreams was followed by the

cupbearer's heartfelt promise of gratitude to remember and reward Joseph for his help. This man, who served in Pharaoh's presence every day, promised to reward Joseph. The right word at the right time and Pharaoh would surely release a slave from prison, even if only to serve in the palace. Anything but prison. After all these years and the endless routines of prison life, out of the blue came a reason for hope. Can you imagine what Joseph felt that day?

Days and weeks later that promise of hope left a bitter after-taste. The forgotten promise served as nothing but a reminder of Joseph's forgotten status. At first the surprise encounter with the baker and cupbearer bore all the signs of divine intervention. Now they were just another tease, another source of false hope. Another reason to cry out, "What are You doing, Lord?"

SURPRISED BY THE PALACE

Do you ever wonder if Joseph counted the passing days with slash marks on the wall of his prison cell? Or do you think he gave up worrying about how long he had been there? Do you think he gave up hoping the cupbearer would keep his promise? Joseph knew his interpretation had been correct, and he knew that every day the cupbearer stood in a position of power and influence. Maybe one day that man would remember his promise. But then again, maybe not. How long can a person cling to a dusty promise?

This emphasis on the passing of time is clear in the text. Chapter 41 begins by forcing us to consider how much time had passed since the incident with the cupbearer—another two years!

Two full years passed before the cupbearer remembered to say anything about Joseph. Two more years! That meant 730 more days of endless hoping—730 mornings awakened to the same stagnant prison smells—730 additional days of wondering, giving up, hoping, remembering—730 days of acute sensitivity to the fact that he had been forgotten. He had no clue as to what was coming down the road. One day led to the next, which led to the next, which led to the next . . . For all Joseph knew, the only thing special about day 730 was that it fell between 729 and 731.

When deliverance finally arrived, it must have been quite a shock. After years spent forgotten in prison, Joseph was whisked from the place of powerlessness into the halls of unbelievable power. After thirteen years as a slave, he was elevated to the position of prime minister. After thirteen years of wondering what his future might hold and serving those who held his future, he became the key to the future of an entire nation. He had maintained his faith in the God of Abraham, Isaac, and his father Jacob. He had lived a life of integrity in spite of opportunities to do otherwise. And now here was the surprise of a lifetime.

Reading the story as it unfolds in Genesis, one might be tempted to say, "Aha! Here is the fairy-tale-like happily-ever-after ending. A Hebrew slave endures a lifetime of hardship and injustice only to emerge on top. Hollywood would line up for the rights to produce his story on film." But stop and ask yourself a few more questions.

Even in this new position of influence, prestige, and prosperity, were the long-lost issues of family and homeland resolved? Was he in a position to find out anything about his family or to send them word about himself? What if his elderly father had passed on during the previous thirteen years? How were the cruel older brothers treating his younger brother Benjamin, the only other child of his mother? Even in the halls of power, was he still not powerless to resolve the deepest sorrows of his life?

Gratefully, the story doesn't end there. Seven years later Joseph and his family enjoyed a tearful reunion and a new beginning. The Scripture portion telling this part of the story is a touching passage filled with tenderness and brokenness as twelve brothers and a brokenhearted father were reconciled to one another. But the miracle of their reunion goes a step deeper. The miracle was not just that God brought them back together, but that God had been working toward this goal all along. For twenty-two years God had been at work behind the scenes to bring about this miraculous deliverance from famine and this family reunion. (From age seventeen to thirty Joseph was a slave and a prisoner. Then after being brought into the palace there were seven years of plenty and two years of drought before Jacob came to Egypt. See Genesis 45:6.)

We walk by faith, not by sight; and to enhance that, it seems that God rarely explains His dealings with our circumstances in full detail. He might give a hint here, point out a little of His handiwork there, or help us recognize how a few circumstances fit together for His purpose. But for Joseph and his family, God revealed the method behind all of the madness. He made it clear to Joseph that all that had happened had been under His watchful eye and orchestrated for this moment. Studying the way God worked in Joseph's life reveals principles to carry us during similar days.

God's Supernatural Work Is Often Carried Out Beyond Our View

A common temptation among us is to assume that what we cannot see cannot be happening, that any work God is not performing where we can see it may not exist. The story of Joseph teaches us differently.

Joseph knew what it was to live in the dark. For twenty-two years he lived cut off from his family and his future, with no prophetic word to which he might cling. He had no means of undoing his predicament. He lived those years one day at a time, blind to the supernatural work and timing of God. He couldn't see the hand of God maneuvering people and circumstances in order to put him in exactly the right place at just the right time.

When we feel cut out of the loop, forgotten by God, and abandoned to the fickle wind of circumstances, the story of Joseph screams out to tell us we are not alone, we are not abandoned, and we are never forgotten. You may not know what God is doing in your life right now, but perhaps you might be encouraged by the list Joseph made of the things God accomplished through his circumstances.

Joseph itemized eight specific ways God used what his brothers meant for evil to accomplish something good (Genesis 45:5-8).

- God *sent me* here *ahead of you*.
- God sent me here to *save the lives of many*.
- God sent me here to *preserve a remnant*.
- God sent me here to *save your lives*.
- God sent me here to *lead a great deliverance*.
- God made me *like a father to Pharaoh*.
- God made me *lord of Pharaoh's entire household*.
- God made me *ruler of all Egypt*.

To these I add two more:

- God sent Joseph to *provide a place where the family of Israel might safely grow into a mighty nation*. A womb in which they could prosper and grow from a family of seventy to a nation of over a million.
- God sent Joseph in order to *fulfill the prophecy* of Genesis 15:13-16. Abraham had been told that his "descendants will be strangers in a country not their own, and they will be mistreated four hundred years. . . . In the fourth generation your descendants will come back here."

Next time you feel forgotten, when your spirit wants to cry

out, "Where are You, Lord? What are You doing?" recall the story of Joseph. Recall the powerful ways God worked behind the scenes in his life. Allow the clarity of God's accomplishments in Joseph's life to serve as a reminder of his commitment to work in your life.

Those Moments That Appear to Be for the Worst May Actually Be for the Best

God sees what we cannot see and knows what we cannot know. Yet, we have a habit of believing that we know more than we do and understand things better than we do. We overestimate the quality of our own perceptions and underestimate the accuracy of God's knowledge of our circumstances.

The only basis at our disposal for knowing whether a situation will turn out for good or for evil is the way it looks at the moment. Yet, even on our best days our understanding is based on a limited number of facts. Only the One who lives outside of time and reigns over all creation is in a position to have perfect understanding. Only the supernatural ability of God is able to bring together all the components of life and work them out for our best interest.

Years and years of disastrous circumstances were all Joseph could see. There was no way for him to see a famine coming down the road. He could have never dreamed of serving in the palace of Egypt as God's emissary for the salvation of a nation. All he could see was one painful turn of events after another. Yet, when the light finally went on, he saw that even those things that appeared to be for the worst were actually for the best.

Even in the Land of Our Suffering God Works Faithfully in the Hearts of His Children

There are two moments late in Joseph's story that allow us to peer into his heart and observe the transformation the grace of

God had accomplished. The first was with the birth of his sons. The second was in his conversation with his brothers after the death of his father.

Sometime after being appointed as prime minister of Egypt, Joseph married an Egyptian girl named Asenath, and they had two sons. Following the custom, Joseph then chose names for his sons that reflected the state of his heart and the circumstances of his life. Now, keep in mind all that had happened. No one could have faulted Joseph for battling with bitterness. But the names he gave to his sons tell us otherwise (see Genesis 41:50-52).

Manasseh, his firstborn, was given a name that sounds like the Hebrew word for "forget"—"because God has made me forget all my trouble and all my father's household." Unbelievable! Joseph's own words tell us that in spite of all that had happened, all the years of disappointment, and all the loneliness he had because he missed his family, God had enabled him to leave his pain behind. Sure, he remembered his experiences; but his pain and sorrow was a thing of the past. God had graciously given him contentment with life as it was.

Ephraim, the second son, was named "twice as fruitful." Joseph had been given the grace to recognize God's active presence and provision even in the land of his suffering. Rather than becoming consumed by what he had given up and what he could never reclaim, the internal work of God in Joseph's heart had given him the ability to dwell on the blessings of his life. He honestly viewed his life as that of a man doubly blessed. During Joseph's sojourn through years of difficult experiences, God had been faithfully at work in his heart.

The second glimpse is just as powerful.

After his father's death and burial, Joseph's older brothers feared that long-held resentment might now be vented (Genesis

50:15). And given the power that Joseph possessed in Egypt, his brothers were rightfully afraid. But nothing of the sort happened.

Although Joseph had the power to exact retribution of the worst kind, he forgave his brothers and explained how God had used the whole circus of events in miraculous ways. In fact, earlier he had not only forgiven them, but he gave them permission to forgive themselves: "Do not be distressed and do not be angry with yourselves" (Genesis 45:5). Because he had forgiven them, they had nothing to fear; there would be no eye for an eye in this case. Because Joseph had discovered that the supernatural plan of God had been carried out behind the scenes, his brothers should forgive themselves, too. What they meant for evil, God meant for good.

Forgiveness is one of the most difficult of all relational tasks. Yet, Joseph extended grace without a grudge. He made no demand for retribution or proof of repentance. He carried no unfinished business over what had happened. And he even went so far as to help them deal with their own need to forgive themselves. Clearly, the tender and faithful work of God had equipped Joseph to deal tenderly with his brothers.

A FINAL HONEST WORD

Bad circumstances do not always resolve themselves in this life. And some circumstances that seem to be resolved are often unexplained. The promise of Joseph's example is not that everything will turn out to be hunky-dory, but that nothing will happen apart from the gaze of our loving Father. Nothing will happen that He will not use for our benefit. No experience will be wasted, but all will contribute to the training of our character and the agenda of His kingdom.

The best answers and the most precious rewards are waiting for us in that place where neither moth nor rust can destroy.

In the presence of our Father, the light of His grace will shed perfect light on all of our unanswered questions.

THE BOTTOM LINE

Whether you can see God at work or not has nothing
to do with whether He is at work or not!

CHAPTER TWELVE

Imprisoned on the Sidelines

I t is not uncommon to feel pushed into limbo during those times when life is up for grabs, when plans fall through, when failure short-circuits our dreams, when jobs don't arrive, when crises hit, and when God says, "Wait." During the types of experiences we have considered throughout this book, there is often a feeling that these conditions have sidelined us from any chance of making an impact for Christ with our lives

When we feel stuck and sidelined, it is easy to question our significance, to wonder what value we could possibly be to God or to anyone else. While each of us desperately desires for our lives to count for something, when we feel sidelined by circumstances, we often also feel sidelined by God and thus insignificant, unusable, weak, unimpressive, helpless.

Had we been David running from King Saul, afraid for our lives and hiding in caves, we would have felt prevented from any chance to accomplish anything for the kingdom. Had we been Joseph and found ourselves stuck in Egypt far away from the people of God, far away from the land of God, we would have felt walled off from any chance to do the work of God.

A frequent companion in the waiting room of life is the devious jester—insignificance. We will now meet a new companion. One who understands but is able to point out new directions. One who can empathize but who will challenge our assumptions. One who will help us press our entire outlook through the filter of eternal truth.

He will offer encouragement and insight, but he will also confront some of our culturally acquired values. He will address our questions of significance and ministry. He will challenge us to view ourselves and our place in God's plans in a new light. And he will open his life to let us learn from his personal journey. He knew what it was to be trapped in situations he didn't ask for, couldn't resolve, and wouldn't wish on his enemies. He experienced seasons of life where there was nothing to write home about and nothing you could call successful or impressive. He is the Apostle Paul.

Now I know that normally we view Paul as someone out of our league. And in many ways he was. He was the greatest missionary the church of Jesus Christ has ever known. He was responsible for most of the New Testament Scriptures. He organized and verbalized some of our most important theology. His legacy is monumental.

However, amidst the awesome testimony of his life we find a cadre of experiences that taught him some of the very same lessons we are so desperate to learn. We find that he endured mishaps and mistreatment—that he was a man, not a superhero. And we find that God's pleasure in using Paul came not from his credentials but from the attitude of his heart.

RETHINKING OUR SUPERHERO THEOLOGY

Ask yourself a few questions: In Christian circles, who is the person that we elevate? When looking for a speaker, what credentials do we look for? When we consider the kind of person God can use, who fits the bill?

Our culture has taught us to elevate the strong and the prominent. To elevate the person who has achieved measurable success or whose appearance defines strength and beauty. We give special audience to those figures who excel in business, sports, or entertainment. In the Christian community we throng around the speaker whose testimony reveals dramatic changes from B.C. to A.C. (before Christ to after Christ)—and the spicier the B.C., the better. We bestow great honor on pastors whose churches achieve numerical prosperity—that is, fast growth and big bucks. We carry on the same pattern found in our culture of giving special honor and a platform of influence to those whose lives appear "together" and "successful."

Please understand—there is nothing wrong with any of these stations in life. In fact, God's creative grace and miraculous work in the lives of people is a cause for praise and celebration. We should rejoice over the athlete who gives his life to Christ, the drug addict who kicks the habit, the church that is knocking down the gates of hell in its own community. We should be excited over the open doors for ministry that accompany notoriety and success in life. We should celebrate these works of God before one another and before God in our worship.

However, when we move from celebrating something special that God has done in the lives of a few to believing that only those with dramatic stories of success and only those whose lives exude strength have anything significant to offer, we short-change the work of Christ in unfortunate ways. When we allow ourselves to believe that broken and hurting people, those who are sidelined by the circumstances of life, have little to offer, we miss the profound opportunities for influence God intends for them. And when we are the ones stuck in that place of distress, we easily miss the astonishing grace and wisdom He offers to us.

You see, God has a way of choosing the weak and the foolish things of this world to confound the wise. He has a way of taking our failures and our foibles and clothing them in His infinite grace. He has a way of shining through us in the midst of our darkest days so others walking through their own difficulties can discover the assurance of God's presence and compassion.

For example, consider Paul. He knew what it was to be stuck on the sidelines, to be weak, to be needy, to struggle with relentless infirmity, to have less than success to boast about. He knew what it was to have a tainted resumé, to possess little that would impress the Roman world. He struggled with the physical infirmity of his thorn in the flesh. He experienced the humiliation of becoming *persona non grata* in more than one city. He endured the public beatings, the shipwrecks, the rejection of the Jewish people, the years spent locked up in prison. Had God called him to minister primarily among the Jews, the pedigree of his past would have found a receptive audience among at least some of them. But no, his calling was to be apostle to the Gentiles, to the people least impressed by his Hebrew training.

The "Dear Abby" column has on several occasions reprinted an interesting essay about a pastoral search committee. This article tells of the committee receiving a unique resumé from a potential minister. This resumé revealed that the minister in question had tremendous educational credentials but no formal pastoral training. It showed that he'd served a number of churches, but the longest he'd ever stayed in a former congregation was three years. In some places he barely stayed more than a few weeks. He caused a riot in one city and had to be lowered over a city wall in order to escape from another. His physical health was not what it used to be, and in fact he suffered a few chronic conditions that neither doctors nor prayer could alleviate. He was not married and had no intentions of becoming so. And in the interest of honesty, he thought the search committee should know that in his earlier days he had participated in the murder of innocent people. Their response? Predictable. The signature at the bottom of the resumé? You guessed it—the Apostle Paul.

Paul's resumé and the content of his writings challenge those culturally acquired values that cause us to believe we must be strong and successful in order to be used significantly by God. Looking at his life challenges the way we debase ourselves during times of weakness and unsettling circumstances. Our cultic worship of image and appearance is not only wrong—it sabotages our outlook on life and ministry. Times of difficulty and need do not automatically relegate us to the sidelines in God's economy. They may actually open up new doors of opportunity.

STUCK IN PRISON DOES NOT MEAN SIDELINED FROM SERVICE

Prison must be the ultimate example of being stuck and sidelined in life. And if you take a man who is passionate toward his calling, zealously aggressive in his work habits, consumed by a burden to touch the lives of people with the Gospel of Jesus Christ—a man who has pursued his calling at full-speed for years—and you put him in prison, you have the Apostle Paul.

Paul was imprisoned a number of times. One of those times began in Jerusalem and ended in Rome approximately five years later. That meant five years of his ministry lost to a prison hiatus. That is in the ballpark of 20 percent of his entire ministry. What kind of ministry can someone have when they are stuck on the sidelines, imprisoned by their circumstances?

This is where Paul begins to challenge our outlook. His

prison years were productive years and lacked the despair we might expect. He shared Christ with the Jewish leaders in Jerusalem, had ongoing conversations about Christ and the Scriptures with Felix, presented his testimony to Caesar, and while in Rome had audiences with local Jews—many of whom gave their lives to the Savior (Acts 28:23-24). Onesimus, the slave of Philemon, gave his life to Christ while imprisoned with Paul. Others like Timothy and Epaphroditus visited Paul in prison and found themselves on the receiving end of his ministry. While in prison Paul used his time to teach and encourage others. He even wrote five New Testament books while in prison.

Ostracized? Insignificant? Sidelined from usefulness? Not hardly. In fact, for 2,000 years his prison letter to the Philippians is one of the New Testament books that Christians have found most encouraging. It was written during the time of his imprisonment, and yet it contains powerful insights about joy, purpose, priorities, peace, contentment, and much more. Two chapters of the book you are reading are devoted to lessons taught in the book of Philippians.

WHEN ISSUES ARE DEEPLY UNSETTLING

Let's ask ourselves the obvious: how do *we* respond to those times in life when circumstances leave us out in the cold? What do we tell ourselves when we are in a position of crisis or helplessness, on hold, stuck, or sidelined? Are we locked out of any chance to make a difference? Are we sidelined with apparently nothing to offer? Paul's example makes a pretty strong argument for the fact that even though we may be disappointed or hurting or worse, God can still use us in profound ways. Even being stuck in prison does not sideline us from effective service.

I have a good friend who suffered a great loss a few years ago. After thirty years of marriage Silvia's husband left her for a woman over twenty years her junior. His decision came as a complete surprise and ripped apart the foundations of her life. Her life had been comfortable, her commitment to Christ sincere, her involvement in the church and in ministry substantial. Nothing prepared her for the spectrum of feelings and the distressing issues that would accompany this trauma in her life. The quicksand of unleashed emotions included a whirlwind of fears and doubts over God's lack of intervention.

Her response was understandable, her painful questioning to be expected. But Silvia was surprised at how completely incapable she felt to serve or minister to anyone else.

A gifted speaker and a caring person, the prison of her pain and the slow, unpredictable progress of her recovery left her feeling that any hope of having a significant ministry was gone. She no longer had the perfect marriage, no longer had an untarnished faith, no longer possessed confident answers for life's difficult demands. Everything was up for grabs. Doubts raged. Anger swelled. Confusion and uncertainty were the order of the day. The woman who had spent most of her adult life giving to others now had nothing to give and was convinced she never would again.

Silvia's experience is not unlike the experience of others whose lives are thrown suddenly and painfully into turmoil. When the calm, predictable pattern of our lives is torn apart, the pain of our experience and the lengthy journey to regain our balance becomes a prison. And there in our prison, because we are no longer in a position of strength or success, because we can no longer invite people to observe the strengths of our lives, we feel abandoned in our insignificance, trapped in obscurity.

Over six years have now passed since the ax fell in my

friend's life. The pain is still very real. The scars remain tender. But she has slowly discovered a new outlook on life. It is a trans-forming outlook. She still wonders about the future, and she wonders whether there will be ministry opportunities for her again. But she has come to discover that God uses cracked pots. She has discovered that the power of God works through us to touch others even when the pieces of our lives are shattered and untidy. There is an intimacy with God in brokenness surpassing anything experienced without it.

THE POWER OF WEAKNESS AND BROKENNESS

I am thinking of my friend as I try to bring these lessons from Paul's life into focus. These are lessons for Silvia and for everyone like her—all whose circumstances have driven them into a quagmire of need. These principles will bring strength and encouragement to everyone who is tempted to feel discarded and useless because of imprisoning circumstances. They are principles to confront the strength and success model we are all affected by or are guilty of promoting. They are principles that will redirect us to the truth of God's Word.

When We Believe God Only Uses the Strong and Successful, We Lose Sight of the Fact That He Loves to Use Broken and Needy People

God has consistently chosen the least likely, the least impressive, the last ones we would normally consider. He doesn't choose us based on our qualifications, but as an extension of His grace.

Paul knew firsthand what it meant to minister from the awkward positions of prison and physical infirmity. But he chose to be unconcerned about impressing people with himself even when he might appear weak (1 Corinthians 2:1-5). He wanted Christ to be seen in him and through him; and if infirmity or calamity could make that happen, so much the better. Even though we may feel trapped in circumstances that don't make sense, Paul makes it clear that we are not cut off from a place of significance.

This is good news and ought to be foundational to our outlook. Here is the principle in his own words:

> *God chose the foolish things of the world to shame the wise;*
> *God chose the weak things of the world to shame the strong.*
> *He chose the lowly things of this world and the despised*
> *things—and the things that are not—to nullify the things*
> *that are, so that no one may boast before him.*
>
> (1 Corinthians 1:27)

When We Buy into the Lie That Our Credentials Are Strength and Success, We Nullify the Sufficiency of Christ

Every facet of the Christian life is built upon the work and grace of Jesus Christ—our salvation, our sanctification, and our place in his kingdom agenda. We have been appointed as ministers of reconciliation not because of who we are or whatever capabilities we possess, but because as sinful, needy people we understand the grace of reconciliation firsthand.

Spiritual gifts are not given to upstanding citizens who demonstrate that they deserve them. Rather, they are distributed throughout the body of Christ, given to every member. Every believer has been privileged to be appointed an ambassador of the Good News. We stand secure in the sufficiency of Christ's saving work, and we are invited to minister to others based on that sufficiency regardless of how our circumstances appear at any given moment.

> *All this is from God, who reconciled us to himself through*
> *Christ and gave us the ministry of reconciliation. . . . And*
> *he has committed to us the message of reconciliation.*

(2 Corinthians 5:18-19)

When We Minister Solely Out of Our Own Strength We Convey the False Notion That People Should Be Like Us

If what we offer to others is merely the example of our own lives and how things have worked out for us, we inadvertently communicate that our lives are the pattern worth following. But *Christ* is the pattern to follow. When something goes wrong, when the ax falls on our own lives, when God sends us through the desert where appearances of strength and success don't exist, what will we have to offer then?

There is so much freedom here. As ambassadors of Christ we don't offer ourselves—we offer Him. We can be honest about our own needs because the validity of our ministry is never based on being without need. We can invite people to join us in our effort to know Him more deeply without constraining them to approach the limits of our strength or progress.

When We Believe That Strength and Success Are Keys to Influence and Ministry We Risk Hiding God's Handiwork Behind Our Own

Paul recognized this risk when he discovered God's ability to use us in our weakness. When we are broken and needy and God works through us, others see His power clearly at work through another human being who is broken and needy like they are. When we portray ourselves strong and successful and without needs, people only see our strength and resourcefulness at work and easily mistake the work of man for the work of God.

When people see us charging forward in the power of our own strength, they evaluate their usefulness based on their ability to duplicate what we do. But when they see God working in us and through us in spite of our weaknesses and needs, they see the power of God who is able to do the same thing in their lives.

> *He said to me, "My grace is sufficient for you, for my power is made perfect in weakness." Therefore I will boast all the more gladly about my weaknesses, so that Christ's power may rest on me.*
>
> (2 Corinthians 12:9)

When We Become Consumed with the Need to Appear Strong or Successful We Lose the Joy and Freedom of Transparency in Christ

Freedom to be honest. Freedom from the pressure to impress. Freedom to be real. Freedom to admit need. Freedom to not have all the answers. Freedom to make mistakes. Freedom to be struggling with some facet of life without incurring judgment. Freedom to be fellow pilgrims in pursuit of intimacy with Christ through the minefields of life. These are wonderful freedoms that we lose if we live under the false notion that we must always put on a happy face.

When we come to understand that the Spirit of God who indwells every believer can use us powerfully in the lives of others, even when our circumstances are less than we hoped for, we discover a whole new level of freedom and honesty. There is no more performing for one another and no more of the empty, sugarcoated conversations that accompany performance. There is freedom to be a fellow struggler. There is the refreshing ability to laugh at ourselves.

And there is a destruction of that sadistic pressure that compounds life's most difficult moments by making us believe that the spiritual well-being of others is solely dependent on how well we hold up under the present catastrophe.

Are you stuck in some type of prison right now? Sidelined by the overwhelming weight of the circumstances you face? Confronted by the frailty of your stamina, wisdom, and faith? If you are, my heart goes out to you. I have no illusion that a few magic words will lighten your load. But I do encourage you to allow the wisdom and testimony of the Apostle Paul to shape your outlook.

Sidelined by circumstances does not mean sidelined by God. Even if the overwhelming nature of what you face right now leaves you feeling as though you have nothing to offer, you are not empty-handed. In the midst of your weakness, the strength of God's handiwork can be seen. In the midst of those days when you have nothing left with which to impress anyone, you have Christ. And He is the impressive one.

I say to you, as I would say to my friend Silvia, the well of God's grace is deeper and fresher than you can possibly imagine. Measure your value and your opportunities by His standard, not those of our culture.

THE BOTTOM LINE

God may very well use us more greatly in our weakness than in our strength and success.

CHAPTER THIRTEEN

When Is It Time to Move Forward?

ave you ever wondered if life wouldn't be much easier if we had a pillar of cloud to lead us by day and a pillar of fire by night? No matter how difficult our situation, at any given moment we would know for sure whether we were to relax and stay put or pack up and move on. We would never be stuck wondering if God wanted us to take matters into our own hands or wanted us to sit tight a bit longer and wait on His timing. We would never doubt whether we were in the right place doing the right thing. And we would never get stuck in the buzz saw of endlessly second-guessing recent events.

Obviously, we don't have a pillar of cloud or of fire. (Probably a good thing for the neighborhood, too.) But that may not put us at a disadvantage. Only one group of people in the history of mankind had such a benefit, and it only lasted for forty years. And if you think about it, the quality of their faith was not much to write home about. The men and women who model genuine faith in the Scriptures walked just as we do—by faith and not by sight. Miraculous signposts are not essential to discovering rest in the Lord when the circumstances of life don't make sense. Vibrant faith is not built on miraculous intervention by God, but on surrendering to the still, small voice of His Spirit.

Yet, the questions persist. When are we to take matters into our own hands, and when are we to continue to wait on our knees? How long should we wait in any given situation? How can we know when God wants us to act and when He wants us to wait? There are times when the wait seems endless, when the path of action is obscured, when anxiety overwhelms us, and life screams for attention. What should we do?

George Müller is famous for his prayers of faith. Early in the years of his ministry, he came to the conviction that he would never speak to another person about his financial need. He made a personal covenant to speak only to the Lord about his needs, believing that the Lord would speak to the right people at the right time. The orphanages he founded were to be run by faith and supplied by God in response to prayer. So pray he did.

God honored Müller's prayer life. Countless stories are told about God's provision for bills due without funds to pay them. Pantries were filled when there was no money to purchase food. Story after story of God's miraculous provision has encouraged and challenged believers for over a century.

Yet, we have to ask ourselves whether or not that is God's pattern for all people at all times. Can God provide in response to prayer alone? Of course He can! His faithfulness is the foundation underlying every lesson in this entire book. There are a great many times where the action called for is the work of prayer. But there are other times when the obedient response is to take immediate action.

Certainly there are times when God wants you to take concrete action. Resting in the Lord by faith does not excuse laziness or refusal to take responsibility. If you find yourself caught in a disconcerting situation but recognize obvious steps that can and should be taken, the question is not if you should act, but simply how to act with wisdom. Go ahead—take action. Respond to the Lord with praise for His provision; get off the couch.

This chapter is not primarily aimed at those times when obvious action is called for—they are self-evident. However, there are other times when life does not make sense and circumstances are beyond your immediate control. Those are the moments when you are desperate to do something, to take some kind of action, to give it your best shot, to do anything but wait passively. Those are the moments we are considering. If we tend to err in those moments, it is usually on the side of impatient action rather than dependent prayer. But how will we know when it is time to get off our knees and do something?

This final chapter is written to pull many of the lessons of this book together, so that you might be able to act with confidence and peace. Our mentor is a young Jewish woman of courageous faith and a resilient spirit.

NOT QUITE A BEAUTY PAGEANT

Esther was a queen, as worthy to sit on the throne of a great nation as any who has ever lived. Yet, she followed a curious path to the palace. A fresh review of her story will set the stage for fresh insights from her faith.

King Xerxes was in the mood for another wife. He already had a substantial harem, but sometime after deposing his former queen he wanted a new one. Don't try to figure him out—it's a long story. His irrationality and explosive anger defy understanding (which explains Esther's fear of him). But we are getting ahead of ourselves.

As you might imagine, a king can find it difficult to meet eligible women. There were no dating services for single kings; so his advisers concocted a plan to hold a national beauty pageant.

Well, perhaps more like a national beauty kidnapping. If you recall the story of Esther, you need to understand that this beauty pageant was nothing like those with which we are acquainted.

The king's officials traveled throughout the kingdom searching for all the "beautiful young virgins" (Esther 2:2). Once found, these women were taken from their villages and brought to the king's harem. I can only imagine that for the majority of these young women, this was a horrifying, even heartbreaking experience. Any supposed glamour was over-shadowed by loneliness, loss, and fear of what lay ahead.

Once in the harem, they received skin treatments and special care to enhance their beauty until it was their turn to be "inspected" by the king. The winner of the contest would become the next queen, while the remainder of the girls would become a permanent part of his harem in case of future "needs."

The *Susa Times* might have run a feature article summarizing this exciting national story with a lead like this: "Young girl from unknown background, possessing exotic beauty and a gentle spirit, has captured the king's heart, stealing the crown from local contestants. Whisked to the capitol, mesmerized by the palace, indulging the finest of delicacies, could this be a young girl's dream come true?"

Or was this a nightmare come to life? If you look closely at the unwritten details of Esther's experience, your stomach will feel the tension. She was just a young girl, in her middle teens. She was given no choice about entering this "contest." She had no choice about being taken from her home. She had no choice about the intimacies of her exposure to the king. She had months of isolation in the harem preparing for her night with Xerxes. Long enough to become anxious, confused, afraid. She was a Jew in a hostile environment chosen to become the wife of an irrational and ruthless man. Facing an unknown future and cut off from her past, she had no choice but to find peace in the Lord, who understood what she could not see.

Meanwhile, back on the streets of the kingdom, strange things were afoot. Haman's vicious plot to exterminate the Jews was written into law. And the law of the Medes and the Persians meant there was no hope of appeal; the king's edict could not be reversed. The death of the Jews was on the calendar and could not be erased.

Into this holocaust in the making, Esther was thrown as the new queen. As queen, Esther had no automatic right to approach the king. She had no guaranteed audience with His Majesty by which she might express her feelings about the coming injustice to the Jews. In fact, Xerxes had no idea she was a Jew!

Should she try to say something? Or should she ask God to use someone who might be in a better position to influence the king? Is this a situation where only the supernatural, direct intervention of God's Spirit could bring about a change in the king's heart? Or is this the kind of situation into which God desires to send a man or woman as His spokesperson? And if God needed to send a person to intervene, how could Esther know she was the right one? Haman had the king's ear, but Esther was just a palace ornament. What was Esther to do?

As a queen with no power, a woman with no right to interfere, a Jewish foreigner despised in the land, and a bedside companion easily replaced, it is easy to imagine Esther reasoning that her place was to wait and to pray. Rules of the kingdom denied her access to the king except at his request. Confronting the king seemed awkward at best, for this plan to destroy the Jews was written into law by his own signature. Throne-room rules meant her death if the king was not in a mood to hear from her. The circumstances did not make sense. What was she to do?

Had not God allowed the Jews to be overrun by the Babylonians and deposed from the Promised Land? Had not

God dispersed them throughout this new land, entwining them with this pagan society? Had not God allowed that wretched beauty pageant? And had not God allowed Esther to be stuck here as the queen in a palace of a sex-crazed ruler? With that kind of track record, it might have been easy for Esther to argue that there was nothing she could do. Just as the entire book of Esther omits the name of God, Esther could have argued that current events omitted any evidence of God too.

But she didn't!

She took action. By faith she stepped out, broached the subject with the king, and saw God extend His hand of deliverance. Her story is a moving, faith-building account. It is also a clear demonstration of the critical issues we must consider when deciding to act during a time of uncertainty.

There are five filters through which we can examine our options when we must decide whether to take direct action or continue waiting in prayer. We see all of these filters in Esther's example. Much like a traffic signal, they have the individual and collective ability to give us a green, yellow, or red light—to tell us to go, to be cautious, or to wait. They also have the ability to bring focus to our actions and thus greater honor to our Lord.

If you are trying to decide what to do, press your decision through these filters. They will help you sort through many of the factors at work and will enable you to study your options with greater clarity.

FILTER #1: MOTIVES

The filter of motives assumes our basic drive to do something physical or concrete, as opposed to patiently waiting in faith. This is the filter that unmasks our rationalized impatience by asking these key questions: Why is it so urgent for me to do something myself? What need is screaming out to be met? What do I want to accomplish so badly? What am I trying to avoid?

With the magnifying glass of honest scrutiny, examine your motives. Not the needs that are superficially apparent, but those personal wants and needs buried beneath the surface. Discovering the needs or wants that you are driven to satisfy will reveal your true motives.

Among the motives driving us to action are some that are positive and admirable. Unfortunately, many others are not. It is these negative motives for which we must be on guard. Most of those tainted motives are familiar to all of us. However, it is still helpful to highlight a few and to ask ourselves if any of these are currently at the helm.

Fear, the chilling feeling that God may not come through in time, argues that we had better handle things ourselves. It makes us doubt God's compassionate interest in our lives.

Impatience, the raw discomfort of being in circumstances beyond our control, takes our eyes off of the One who holds the universe together.

Envy is the ruthless desire to acquire possessions or circumstances that others appear to have. The problem with envy is that it rarely looks beneath the surface; it sees only what it wants to see.

Pride is that insidious companion that causes us to stumble over concerns about what others might think when they see the circumstances we are in. The desire to impress, to posture ourselves in order to look good at all times, to avoid any appearance of weakness or need—these all spawn from the cesspool of pride.

Control is that insatiable desire to have the circumstances of life under our thumb. We want things, and even people, under our control so that there are no surprises, and worse, so that we are free from needing help—from God or anyone else.

There are other possible motives, but you get the idea.

Which of these compel you to take action? Which deceive you into believing there are valid reasons why you cannot continue to rest in the Lord with circumstances the way they are? Should you find that your compelling drive to take action is fueled by unhealthy motives, pull back on the reins. You are facing a red light.

Esther's character and courage were amazing. Facing grave personal risk and the imminent extermination of her people—read, her family and friends—she wisely and carefully worked through the issues. She knew that the king's order to "destroy, kill and annihilate all the Jews" would include her if her background were discovered (Esther 3:13). She might have easily opted to continue hiding her identity. Instead, she chose a course of action that was anything but self-serving.

You catch a glimpse of her motives during a discussion with her Uncle Mordecai. When he offered the suggestion that perhaps she was brought to the palace "for such a time as this" (Esther 4:14), Esther's actions showed her agreement. She did not decide to approach the king for some selfish goal but because she recognized the need of her people. She acknowledged the fact that she may have been called by God for a unique purpose. A purpose she had never considered until now. A course of action whose outcome was anything but guaranteed. Her willingness to serve as God's tool with no strings attached led her onto a path of great risk.

FILTER #2: CONTENTMENT

This second filter focuses on the state of our heart and our ability to rest in the Lord. It confronts our tendency to seek contentment in circumstances or relationships and reminds us to draw strength and stability from God's presence and provision.

One question brings the whole issue of contentment into

focus: Will I be OK no matter what happens, or is my well-being wrapped up in the outcome of my circumstances?

Without any guarantees, without any cosmic sign of divine approval, Esther went ahead with a plan that could have easily failed. Even though failure would cost her life, she went forward, content with whatever outcome God would allow. She said, "I will go to the king, even though it is against the law. And if I perish, I perish" (Esther 4:15).

We might paraphrase her decision as, "I will do what I believe is right. God may have placed me here in this position for just this purpose. However, if I am mistaken, I will not blame God for my mistake, and I will not doubt my place in His kingdom. If the king demands my life for entering his presence without being requested, then I will give up my life doing what I believed to be the best way to serve my people. My motives are in the right place. I am content to act without any guarantee of the outcome."

Ask yourself the questions of contentment. Do you require a change of circumstances before you can again experience that calm center inside? Do you feel compelled to take action because you simply cannot stand the turmoil any longer? Or are you at rest, content deep down inside, regardless of whether life begins to make sense in the immediate future or not?

If this filter raises a red flag and you are dependent on circumstances to make you content, taking action will do very little in the long run. It's time to relearn the lesson that could make Paul content even in prison—namely, that the daily, enabling power of Christ is your only hope.

FILTER #3: PRAYER

You would think that the need for prayer goes without saying. Unfortunately, it is very easy for God's people to talk about prayer and about matters in need of prayer, but to then move on without taking the time to pray. It is easy to discuss needs for prayer over the phone without taking those requests to the Throne. It is as if we feel vicariously satisfied by the discussion of prayer even though we have not actually engaged in prayer.

Hopefully your experience is different, but I have known of prayer chains that diligently pass requests along and get so caught up in the mechanics of the telephone chain that very little actual prayer is offered to God. I have participated in prayer meetings and Bible studies that take extensive time to share requests with one another, only to find that they had little time remaining to do the actual work of prayer.

James 4:2 nails us on this note. James notices how circumstances and desires can make us uptight, and he identifies the connection with our prayer habits:

> *You want something but don't get it. You kill and covet, but you cannot have what you want. You quarrel and fight. You do not have,* because you do not ask God *(emphasis added).*

When life doesn't make sense and we are overwhelmed with the needs at hand, it is easy to recognize our need for the renewing work of Christ. It is easy to share those needs with people we trust. And it is easy to just *not* get around to doing the actual work of prayer.

Thinking about prayer is not prayer. Talking about prayer is not prayer. Sharing needs for prayer with others may be an essential part of preparing for prayer; but until we share those needs directly with God, we have not prayed.

Prayer is entering God's presence and engaging Him with our concerns. This requires doing the work necessary to set other things aside—physically or mentally—so that "in everything, by prayer and petition, with thanksgiving, [we may] present [our] requests to God" (Philippians 4:6). It is approaching "the throne of grace with confidence, so that we may receive mercy and find grace to help us in our time of need" (Hebrews 4:16).

When Esther faced the reality of what lay ahead, she set aside three days for prayer and fasting. (Esther 4:16 tells us of her call for a three-day fast, and although the text does not mention prayer, I am taking the liberty of surmising that because of the spiritual nature of the fast and the clear fact that they were looking to the Lord for a miraculous work, prayer was a major component of this fast.) She called on all the Jews living in the area of Susa and all of her maids to join in the fast. She did more than report the need for prayer. She did more than ask others to pray while she tackled the situation at hand. She and Mordecai set the pace for a three-day movement of prayer.

There's nothing mysterious about this filter of prayer. Just consider the simple, straightforward question, "Have you prayed aggressively and substantially about the circumstances and the decisions you are facing?"

FILTER #4: TIME

If you have worked through the filters of motive, contentment, and prayer, you are more than halfway home. Time is the fourth filter in the decision-making process. Unfortunately, it is probably the most ambiguous of the lot. Nebulous as it may be, time is still a valid filter for consideration.

Ask yourself this simple, clarifying question: Have I given the Lord time to answer, time to work His plans?

At the outset of this book we said waiting on the Lord means placing circumstances, desires, and people in the Lord's hands and then resting in His ability to work things out in His way and in His time. Now we must square off against the villain of time again.

Time has been the underlying enemy throughout this book. Generally speaking, the more time that passes by, the more intensely we struggle with our circumstances. The longer things go unresolved, the greater our eagerness to do something *now*. The longer our dilemmas appear to stretch into the future, the more uptight we are in the present. As we struggle we keep coming back to the time factor.

Granted, Esther did not set aside large quantities of time. She fasted and prayed for three days; after that she gave God room to work for another twenty-four hours before taking action regarding the plight of her people. Four days may not be much, but when your life and the lives of all your family and friends are at stake, even ten minutes can be excruciating.

Even more impressive is the fact that during this four-day delay, Esther placed matters completely in the Lord's hands. There was no testing of the waters behind the king's back. There were no hints of something important coming. There were no messengers or gifts sent to the king to warm his heart before the big day. She and all the Jews in the capital city prayed and waited. They gave the Lord time to answer and to work.

Put yourself in her shoes. I know that if it had been me, I would have spent the bulk of those days pondering, even obsessing, over all the options. I would have rehearsed my words and planned every movement, every step in my course of action. Then when finally I entered the presence of the king, I probably would have exploded with everything all at once. Had I kept my mouth closed, the king would still have recognized the brewing storm because of my countenance. But Esther was different.

With calmness, grace, contentment, and confidence oozing from her pores, she invited the king to a banquet. At the banquet she refrained from spilling the beans, instead inviting him back a second day and thereby increasing the importance of the message she wished to bring. She was giving God time.

Here you catch a glimpse of God's sense of humor. God did a miracle in a down-to-earth manner. Xerxes couldn't sleep that night; so he called for something to make him drowsy. He was so desperate, he began reading from the record book of his reign—the congressional record of his kingdom! Lists. Names. Places. Endless minutiae. It's the kind of stuff that could put *anyone* to sleep. Then he saw it.

Buried in the records of his reign was the tale of the man Mordecai, Esther's uncle, who had earlier uncovered a plot to assassinate the king. Of all the volumes Xerxes could choose from—of all the pages he could start reading—of all the things he could do on a sleepless night—he just "happened" to stumble onto the account of Mordecai. This was the same Mordecai whom Haman intended to hang the next day. And this was the same Haman who was responsible for planning the annihilation of the Jews.

Who in their right mind would plan to murder the man who saved the king's life? Could there be an easier way to incur a potentate's wrath?

Esther had given God time. And God was working.

By the time Xerxes arrived for his banquet the following day, the snowball of God's intervention was barreling down upon Haman. God had creatively used a king's insomnia and the risk-taking obedience of a woman named Esther to demonstrate His power and presence to a people long isolated in their exile.

Have you given God time?

Waiting is not laziness. Bold faith may mean giving God more time just as often as it means taking a risk now. Only you will know if you have given God time to act in response to your prayers. If your heart is tender toward the things of God, His Spirit will be able to guide you into the right timing.

FILTER #5: REST

Let's assume that you have examined your motives and found they are in order. You are genuinely content with whatever agenda God has in store. You have prayed diligently and perhaps even enlisted the prayer support of others. And you have given God time to intervene in His own way. If you have a green light in all four of these areas, you probably have the freedom to step out and take action as you see fit.

The final filter is one to guide you on the go. It is the filter of rest. Maybe you have noticed that when we finally get to take action after a long period of waiting on the Lord, all the anxiety returns. Once we begin to take action, it is tempting to reclaim full responsibility for the outcome of events. Yet, the very lesson God has worked so hard to teach us during the times of uncertainty is that He intends for us to rest in Him and in His ability to work.

Therefore, whether you are taking action after a long period of waiting or you have been chest-deep in the waters of activity for a long time, ask yourself the question at the heart of this filter of rest: Am I resting in the Lord and in His ability, or am I assuming that everything depends on me and my ability?

Every one of the men and women whose lives we have examined has exemplified this quality of rest. Even in the most stress-filled times they demonstrated the presence of a calm center. We see the presence of peace, contentment, trust, and even praise as they moved through uncertain times.

Jehoshaphat was busy singing songs of praise as he led the people over the hill to battle at En Gedi.

Abraham was calm and certain as he walked with Isaac up the mountain to that altar of sacrifice.

David refused to touch the life of Saul, even when the evil king's life was placed in his hands. It wasn't God's time, and David was willing to wait.

Paul wrote about contentment and joy while chained to a Roman guard.

Esther strode calmly into the throne room of the king and possible death.

Jeremiah preached with conviction even when God's Word brought him ridicule and imprisonment.

Joseph served with such integrity and obedience that even his guardians were drawn to the beauty of his character.

And there were others too. *Daniel* walked into the lion's den calmly aware of God's faithful presence. *Shadrach, Meshach, and Abednego* were content to give their lives in the furnace if God chose not to rescue them. *Stephen* continued to witness to his killers as they stole his life away. *Paul and Silas* sang hymns while their lives were at stake in prison.

All these men and women of God portray people at rest. Their circumstances called for anything but rest, and yet they possessed a calm center cultivated by the conviction that the Lord could be trusted to work things out in His way and in His time.

Ask yourself this final question: Can I take action myself and in my spirit remain at rest, giving the Lord freedom to work things out in His way and in His time?

If the answer is no, maybe you should reconsider your course of action. If the answer is yes, you have another green light.

Line these five filters up one after another and peer through them. If any one of them signals a red light, you would be wise to wait longer. On the other hand, if all five of these filters signal a green light, then go ahead. Take action. Allow God to direct you and redirect you as you move forward. Allow God to bring about a solution from some source you never considered. Allow God, should He decide to put another wrench in the works, to perform surgery on your character at a deeper level. In short, if you have the go-ahead on all levels, then move ahead by faith. Trust God in your time of action as deeply as you trusted Him in your time of inaction.

The key to rest is the posture of your spirit, not the condition of your circumstances. Waiting on the Lord is more than holding on through endless delay; it is a quality of life characterized by active dependence on Him. He "who is able to do immeasurably more than all we can ask or imagine" is able to be trusted with every unsettling nuance in our lives (Ephesians 3:20-21). He may not always work the way we wish. In fact, He may rarely work the way we wish. But He will always give us Himself, and He is enough! His mercies are new every morning (Lamentations 3:22-23).

THE BOTTOM LINE

Whether we are kneeling in prayer or spinning in a whirlwind, rest results from the posture of our spirit, not control or knowledge of the future.

Epilogue

If you have seen many Hollywood westerns, whether on TV or at the movies, you'll be familiar with the following scene: Apprehended for crimes he may or may not have committed, a cowboy's hands are tied to one end of a long rope. The other end of the rope is knotted to the saddle on a horse. The rider of that horse spurs his steed into a gallop, while the cowboy tries with all his strength to run fast enough to keep up.

The viewer knows there is no way the cowboy at the end of his rope can remain on his feet very long. But we all know he will try. If we were in his situation, we would do the same. However, sooner or later he will lose the battle.

Don't take that analogy too far, but when life doesn't make sense it is easy for us to feel like that cowboy who is desperately trying to stay on his feet. Running as hard as we can, frantically trying to maintain our balance, every step increases our fear that we will lose the battle, take a nosedive into the rocks and cactus, and be dragged to our destruction.

Rest in the Lord is possible even when life doesn't make sense. When we are being pulled in a multitude of directions at the same time, it is still possible to cultivate a calm center. When the future—or the present—looks dark and foreboding, when there is no light to be found in our circumstances, hope may still be found in Him who is the light of the world. The testimony of Scripture and of the people of God throughout the ages tells us that peace and rest are possible.

Hear God's offer one last time. Written into a song that the people of God might sing to themselves and to one another,

Isaiah captured the heart of our need and the heart of God's offer. Perhaps these words would serve you well as the substance of your meditation during dark and unsettling days.

> *Do you not know?*
>> *Have you not heard?*
> *The LORD is the everlasting God,*
>> *the Creator of the ends of the earth.*
> *He will not grow tired or weary,*
>> *and his understanding no one can fathom.*
> *He gives strength to the weary*
>> *and increases the power of the weak.*
> *Even youths grow tired and weary,*
>> *and young men stumble and fall;*
> *but those who hope in the LORD*
>> *will renew their strength.*
> *They will soar on wings like eagles;*
>> *they will run and not grow weary,*
> *they will walk and not be faint.*

(Isaiah 40:28-31)

And one last time:

> *Since ancient times, no one has heard,*
>> *no ear has perceived,*
> *no eye has seen any God besides you*
>> *who acts on behalf of those who wait for him.*

(Isaiah 64:4)

The Bottom Line

1. Waiting on the Lord is the timeless answer to our contemporary need for rest in the midst of life's storms.

2. "Stand at the crossroads and look; ask for the ancient paths, ask where the good way is, and walk in it, and you will find rest for your souls!" (Jeremiah 6:16)

3. Contrary to popular opinion, prayer is the most tangible and practical thing we can do in the face of a crisis.

4. When you wait on the Lord for what you cannot do, you discover just how much He can do!

5. Peace comes when we relinquish ownership of what we face to the One who has unlimited ability, inexhaustible resources, and impeccable timing.

6. Trusting God because a desirable outcome seems probable is not really trusting *Him* at all— it is trusting in probabilities.

7. Contentment is not the product of heroic self-effort, but is found only in the daily, enabling power of Christ.

8. The character of God is never synonymous
   with the quality of our circumstances. God is good,
   even when life stinks.

9. Far from being a sign of disapproval, seasons of
   silence may even be indicators of God's pleasure.

10. God loves us too much to take anything less than
    an aggressive role in the development of our
    character.

11. Whether you can see God at work or not has
    nothing to do with whether He is at work or not!

12. God may very well use us more greatly in our
    weakness than in our strength and success.

13. Whether we are kneeling in prayer or spinning in a
    whirlwind, rest results from the posture of our spirit,
    not control or knowledge of the future.